# FINDING
# THE
# PLOT

# FINDING THE PLOT

## 100 GRAVES TO VISIT BEFORE YOU DIE

### ANN TRENEMAN

ILLUSTRATIONS BY REBECCA BROWN

/R/

# FINDING THE PLOT

## 100 GRAVES TO VISIT BEFORE YOU DIE

### ANN TRENEMAN

ILLUSTRATIONS BY JOHN JENSEN

The Robson Press

First published in Great Britain in 2013 by
The Robson Press (an imprint of Biteback Publishing)
Westminster Tower
3 Albert Embankment
London SE1 7SP
Copyright © Ann Treneman 2013

ISBN 978-1-84954-195-4

10 9 8 7 6 5 4 3 2 1

A CIP catalogue record for this book is available from the British Library.

Set in Baskerville

Printed and bound in Great Britain by
CPI Group (UK) Ltd, Croydon CR0 4YY

MIX
Paper from
responsible sources
FSC
www.fsc.org   FSC® C020471

# CONTENTS

# GEOGRAPHICAL GUIDE TO GRAVES

# INTRODUCTION

I know what you are thinking. You want to know, as did almost everyone else who I have told about this book, how I got the idea for it and how I picked the graves. So first, the idea. In my day job, when I'm not running around cemeteries, I am the political sketchwriter for *The Times* and, just before the 2010 election, I was chatting to an MP named Tony Wright who is, unlike some politicians, one of the good guys. He was standing down as Labour MP for Cannock Chase and we started talking about Birmingham. Did he know, I asked, that the inventor of the phenomenally success-ful board game Cluedo had lived in Bromsgrove? I had done a story on the man, with the marvellous name of Anthony E. Pratt, and had tracked down his grave which, at the time, also seemed under threat from the Brum mole population. 'Ah,' said Tony, 'that's interesting; I don't think anyone has ever written a book about the best graves in Britain.'

'Hmmm,' I said, 'well maybe that would be fun.'

It is now almost four years later and, though it's been fun, it's also involved a lot of what I call 'graving' (not to be confused with gravy, by the way), which I think should be a new verb.

So how did I choose them? The first was easy. That was Cluedo inventor Mr Pratt. So then, only ninety-nine to go. I learned, pretty quickly, that there actually had been many books published on famous graves, though none in this format. I talked to just about everyone I met about their favourite graves (I am sure you can see how popular I was making myself). Plus there were my personal quirks and favourites. I also looked through books and, feeling a bit like some sort of intrepid Victorian explorer, made my way through the extraordinary database of 4,500 British graves listed by the website Find A Grave. These were my basic rules for choosing:

- The list had to be eclectic and everyone on it had to be interesting. I mustn't let my personal obsessions intrude too much though readers will be able to discern some obvious ones (step forward James Bond).
- I had to include iconic, historical and architectural graves. So I had one for the Beatles (Eleanor Rigby) and the great plague (the Hancock family in Eyam). There are also graves that I chose purely for what they looked like, but I soon found that people with interesting graves were exactly that themselves.
- They couldn't be too depressing or upsetting. I put very few recent graves in my list and I thought long and hard about those that I did. For instance, I figure that Philip Gould, the political strategist who died in 2011 and wrote a book about his experience of dying, would actually want to be on the list. I was also wary of murder victims. This book is about lives, not deaths.
- The graves had to be accessible, if only for a few days a year. This ruled out the likes of the Royal Mausoleum at Frogmore, which has been closed for years but, as a way of doing Queen Victoria, I did the grave of her servant (and who knows what else), John Brown.
- The graves should, in general, not be expensive to visit. There were a few exceptions. I had to include at least one grave each in the great soaring necropolises of Westminster Abbey and St Paul's. I don't begrudge the small fee to enter the likes of Highgate or, indeed, the charge for Newstead Abbey, where the grave of Byron's dog resides in full glory.

- About half of the graves should be in or around London. This was both practical, in the sense that I think many readers will be visiting London, and sensible because I think that per square mile London has the most interesting dead people of anywhere in the world.
- I had to visit them. This might sound basic but you'd be surprised how easy it is to convince yourself that this would not be necessary. In a perfect world, for instance, the island of Iona would be on this list. But I just didn't have the time to go and swim out there (that's a joke).

Now, looking over the 100, I think I have stuck to my rules overall. I must admit that, as I look over the list, I remain intrigued by every name but I can also see some faults. God, there are a lot of Victorians (but then they were the ones who invented the modern-day cemetery). And I have failed in some areas of geography (Edinburgh, among others, please forgive). Indeed, the one thing that I know as I write this introduction is that everyone who reads this book will want to add a grave or two. I considered quite seriously leaving the last of the 100 slots blank for you to fill in. But then I found Fred in deepest Beckenham (Frederick York Wolseley was the last grave I did) and I knew I couldn't leave it blank.

*Ann Treneman*
London
July 2013

*Jean François Gravelet or 'Blondin', Kensal Green Cemetery*

# CENTRAL LONDON

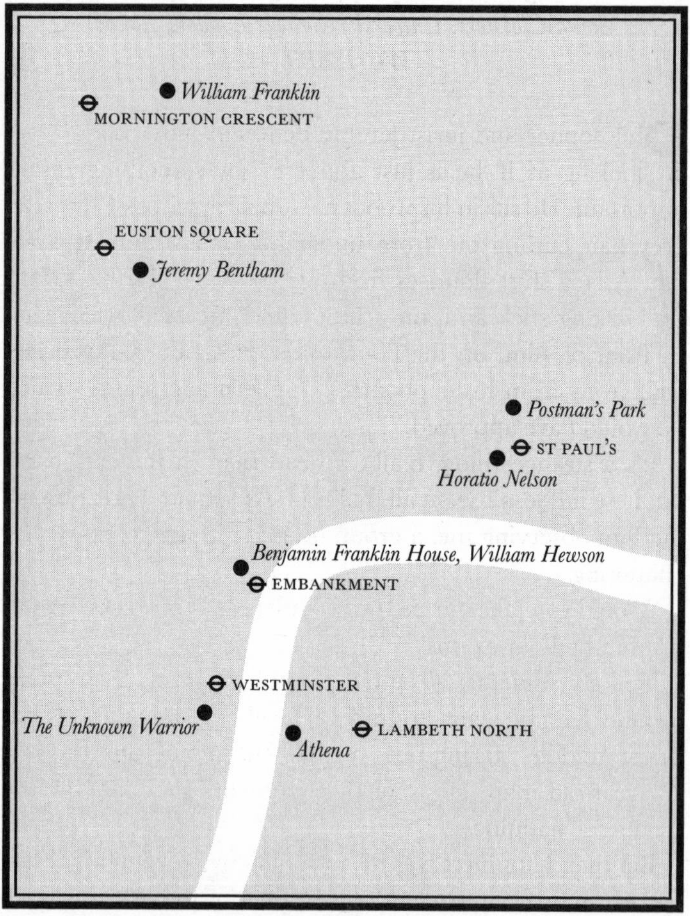
William Franklin
MORNINGTON CRESCENT
EUSTON SQUARE
Jeremy Bentham
Postman's Park
ST PAUL'S
Horatio Nelson
Benjamin Franklin House, William Hewson
EMBANKMENT
WESTMINSTER
The Unknown Warrior
Athena
LAMBETH NORTH

# JEREMY BENTHAM

## AUTO-ICON
### 15 February 1748–6 June 1832
*South Cloisters, University College London, London*
*WC1E 6BT*

**P**hilosopher and jurist Jeremy Bentham stares out at you, looking as if he is just about to say something rather important. He sits in his wooden cupboard, wisps of his (real) grey hair curling out from under his wide-brimmed straw hat. A lacy shirt flounces from his waistcoat. By his side is his walking stick and, on a little table, his small spectacles. In front of him, on the floor, three decals of X-rayed feet walk away from his cupboard, a modern addition of which he would have approved.

It's a strange thing, really, a dead man in the cupboard, but here it doesn't seem all that odd. As I stand there, observing him observing me, a group of students arrive, noisy and chattering.

'Would you take our picture with Jeremy?' one asks. 'We've just finished our exams!'

The six students, all about twenty, giggle as they group around Jeremy, arms around each other's shoulders. Right in the middle, staring out, very much part of the fun, is a 181-year-old man. He is, at that moment, quite literally the picture of happiness.

But then happiness was his raison d'être. For Jeremy (I feel we are on first-name terms) is the father of the philosophy of utilitarianism, whose fundamental precept is that the greatest happiness for the greatest number determines what is right or wrong. His ambition was to create a 'Pannomion', a complete utilitarian code of law. He spent years working on his vision of a prison building called the Panopticon.

Born wealthy, he was a child prodigy who trained as a lawyer but never practised, instead spending his life criticising how the legal system worked. His many students included John Stuart Mill. He was a man ahead of his time and University College London claims him as its 'spiritual father' in that, like Bentham, its policy was (and is) to admit all, regardless of race, creed, wealth or political belief. An obsessive writer who almost never finished anything himself, Jeremy, who died at the age of eighty-three, left behind 30 million words, most of which reside not that far from his skeleton, and are still being organised.

'Auto-icon is a word I have created,' he wrote. 'It is self-explanatory.' Jeremy's vision was that we would all become Auto-icons, thus doing away with burials. He wrote:

> In general, in the present state of things, our dead relations are a source of evil – and not of good. The fault is not theirs but ours. They are nuisances – and we make them so: they generate infectious disease; they send forth the monster Typhus to destroy; we may prevent this. Why do we not prevent it?

He explains that in his will he had left his body for dissection, but that afterwards the head would be preserved – he was enthusiastic about a Maori process of mummification. The idea was that, eventually, everyone would embrace Auto-iconism. He wrote:

> Our churches are ready-provided receptacles for Auto-icons, provided for all classes, for rich and poor. There would no longer be needed monuments of stone or marble – there would be no danger to health from the accumulation of corpses – and the use of churchyards would gradually be done away with. It would diminish the horrors of death, by getting rid of its deformities: it would leave the agreeable associations,

and disperse the disagreeable. Of the *de mortuis nil nisi bonum*, it would be the best application: it would extract from the dead only that which is good – that which would contribute to the happiness of the living. It would set curiosity in motion – virtuous curiosity. Entire museums of Auto-icons would be formed.

That was the vision. The reality is that today most people think Auto-icons are something to do with cars. Indeed Jeremy is the only Auto-icon that I know. He was originally kept by his disciple Thomas Southward Smith. His experiment at mummification, using the Maori methods of placing the head under an air pump over sulphuric acid and drawing off the fluids, was successful – but gruesome. Jeremy's real head looks distinctly scary and so it was decided to give the Auto-icon a wax head, with his own hair.

Jeremy went to 'live' at UCL in 1850. For some years, his real head was displayed in the same case – between Jeremy's feet – but students from rival institutions kept stealing it, holding it hostage. The head has now been locked away. Jeremy himself would never want to be locked away. Indeed it is said that he sometimes attends UCL board meetings (where he is listed as 'present – not voting'). What struck me, when I visited him, was that just by existing, he has provided much happiness to those who live with him every day. And that, of course, was the idea.

# WILLIAM FRANKLIN

## SON OF BENJAMIN FRANKLIN
**1730 (date unknown)–17 November 1814**
*The Hardy Tree, Old St Pancras Churchyard, Pancras Road,*
*London NW1 1UL*

# WILLIAM HEWSON

## MEDICAL PIONEER
**14 November 1739–1 May 1774**
*St Martin-in-the-Fields (grave lost), Trafalgar Square, London*
*WC2N 4JJ*

*Plus his bodies under Benjamin Franklin House,*
*36 Craven Street, London WC2N 5NF*

.**I**f this story weren't true, I wouldn't believe it. It involves six
men – four famous, two illegitimate – and a very tall, thin
house built in 1730 at 36 Craven Street in London. Indeed my
story begins with a trip to that house, now a museum, and the
only surviving home on any continent of Benjamin Franklin,
the brilliant polymath and American Founding Father, who
lived there as a lodger on and off from 1757  until 1775. He
was extraordinarily engaged in life, fascinated by everyone
and everything, printer, diplomat, revolutionary and inventor
of the Franklin stove, the lightning rod, the glass harmonica
and, of course, bifocals. As you negotiate the steep steps, the
walls painted now, as then, in a shade called Franklin Green,
it is quite hard to imagine that Ben once sat gloriously naked
by the large first-floor sash windows, 'air bathing'. It wouldn't
happen today.

For some of his time there, he would have been accompanied

by William Franklin, his illegitimate but acknowledged son. William was born in 1730 in Philadelphia, his mother unknown. But he was raised by Ben and his common-law wife, Deborah Read. They were never able to marry for the simple reason that she already was – or could have been. It seems that Ben had proposed when he was just seventeen, and she fifteen, but this was rejected by her father. So instead she married another man who promptly ran off to Barbados with her dowry and never returned, thus tying her to him for life.

The Franklins, father and son, spent a great deal of time in London (Deborah, afraid of sea travel, never visited). William got his law degree and had his own illegitimate son named, somewhat confusingly, William Temple Franklin. In 1763 Ben managed, via contacts with the British government, to have his son appointed as Lieutenant Governor of New Jersey, a role that he relished but which, in the end, would be the undoing of him and his father.

Ben kept up an exhausting pace, both intellectual and physical. He really was one of those people who could never let anything be. (In 1768, while at Craven Street, he developed a new phonetic alphabet which got rid of c, j, q, w, x and y. As you do.) His main role may have been as a colonial agent, mediating between Britain and America, but he was a whirlwind of activity and endeavour – writing, debating, experimenting, eating, drinking, entertaining the likes of Thomas Paine and Edmund Burke, and in general living life to the full. It sounds a slightly crazed household, with his landlady Margaret Stevenson and her daughter Mary (who was known as Polly) making up what seems almost another family for him. Things got even busier in 1770 when Polly married William Hewson, a medical pioneer, surgeon and anatomist whose outstanding work on blood means he is now sometimes called the 'father of haematology'. With Franklin's help, Hewson set up an anatomy school and lecture theatre at Craven Street.

What this actually entailed would have remained buried history if it were not for the fact that, in 1997, a restoration project was embarked on at Benjamin Franklin House. And guess what they found in the back garden? 'Stop Press! Bones found at No. 36! Stop Press!' cried the newsletter. And not just any bones but 200-year-old ones from at least ten human skeletons, some of which were children. The police were notified. A report from the London *Evening Standard* in February 1998 notes: 'Most of the bones show signs of being dissected, or cut, while one skull has been drilled with several holes, suggesting it was used for early experiments in trepanning – a surgical procedure to remove bone from the skull. The main suspect in the mystery has emerged as Dr William Hewson.' It goes on to note the bodies would have been snatched from local graveyards, an illegal practice for which the penalty was death or deportation. Mr Hewson and his students were thought to have carried out the 'experiments' in the basement kitchens.

At Craven Street today you can stand in the basement and look down through a 'window' into the ground. This is the burial pit where, in total, 1,200 pieces of bone were found. There are display cases of skulls with holes drilled into them. It really is quite surreal. I tried to imagine the scene in the 1770s. There was Benjamin Franklin, almost electrocuting anyone crazy enough to help him with his electricity experiments, and there was William Hewson, smuggling in bodies, carving them up, and digging deep in the back garden to bury them. What a place! And, of course, there is every chance that Franklin, pathologically curious, attended these dissections. But then, in 1774, at the age of thirty-four, Hewson cut himself while dissecting a putrid body, contracted septicaemia and died. He was buried in St Martin-in-the-Fields church, just around the corner on Trafalgar Square.

All of this and war too! The next year Benjamin Franklin
would return to the Colonies, giving up on peace with
England. By this time, in May 1775, the war had started.
Benjamin would become a deeply respected and loved
Founding Father, his kindly face as famous now as it was then.
But a story that is much less known is that his illegitimate son,
still serving as Royal Governor in New Jersey, stayed loyal
to the King. William Franklin was deposed in 1776, imprisoned in Simsbury Mines, a cavern seventy feet underground,
before he fled to New York, which was still occupied by the
British. There he became a royalist guerrilla, launching
raids into neighbouring states. When the British troops left,
William Franklin left with them. He settled in London and
never returned.

He and his father were never reconciled. Ben was uncom-
promising in his position that a Loyalist should not be given
amnesty or compensation. He left William nothing in his
will except for some territory in Nova Scotia, noting that, if
Britain had won the war, he would have had nothing to leave
him anyway. He dedicated his autobiography to him but then
never mentioned him in it. It seems there is no bit of this tale
without a twist, for Benjamin Franklin had found out about
his (illegitimate) grandson William Temple and brought him,
at the age of thirteen, to Philadelphia to live with him. Later,
William Temple would return to England to live with his
father (and, of course, have his own illegitimate daughter!).

Benjamin Franklin died in 1790. William, who remained
a leading Loyalist in London and never tired of the idea of
reconciling with the States, died in 1813 at the age of eighty-
two. The *Oxford Dictionary of National Biography* says he was
buried in St Pancras Old Church Cemetery. So I went to St
Pancras to find him: it is a gem of a place, tucked away around
the back of the British Library and the railway station. The
church, possibly dating from the fourth century, is simple,

small and intimate – a true joy. The churchyard is more a park with a smattering of graves to break up the landscape. I dragooned someone named Tim, a volunteer guide, and we zoomed round, looking for William Franklin's grave.

We found several others on the way. In a neat bit of fate, it turns out that Charles Dickens had a link to this place. He identified this graveyard by name in *A Tale of Two Cities* as the location of bodysnatching to provide corpses for dissection at medical schools! It was here that Jerry Cruncher and his son came 'fishing', armed with a spade. Shades of William Hewson, in every sense. And among the graves we did find was that of William Jones, headmaster of Wellington House Academy, who died in 1836. The gravestone identifies him as 'master of a respectable school'. That, of course, is not how Dickens, a day pupil there, remembers it, calling him 'by far the most ignorant man I have ever had the pleasure to know'. Mr Jones was also 'one of the worst-tempered men perhaps that ever lived'. Mr Creakle, the ferocious headmaster in *David Copperfield*, was based on William Jones.

A main attraction of this graveyard is what is now called The Hardy Tree, a strange sight in which the roots of a giant ash tree have grown up between what seems like hundreds of old gravestones. It turns out that Thomas Hardy, before he was a writer, was an architecture student. In the 1860s, the railway line was due to be built over part of the church-yard, and Hardy's firm was given the job of exhuming the bodies and moving the gravestones. This he did, planting the tree as a sign of life among so many dead. It is believed that among these stones, packed round, hugging this tree so tight, is the tombstone of William Franklin.

So let's take stock. Our first death was William Hewson, who was buried in St Martin-in-the-Fields but whose grave has now been lost (though there is a fascinating series of tomb-stones which have been saved through the ages on display in the crypt). It seems that William Franklin's grave is also lost, with his stone probably moved to the Hardy Tree. And *his* illegitimate son, William Temple, who became Benjamin Franklin's literary executor, is buried at Père Lachaise in Paris. So we are left with many bodies and no epitaphs (except for the deeply unexceptional Mr Creakle, I mean Jones). But this feels like a tale in need of an epitaph and so I bring you instead some words from Ben, who famously said: 'I wake up every morning at nine and grab for the paper. Then I look at the obituary page. If my name is not on it, I get up.'

His grave in Philadelphia at Christ Church burial ground has just names and dates – a strange state of affairs for this most loquacious of men. So here then is this mock epitaph, composed when he was young:

THE BODY OF B. FRANKLIN

PRINTER;

LIKE THE COVER OF AN OLD BOOK,

ITS CONTENTS TORN OUT,

AND STRIPT OF ITS LETTERING AND GILDING,

LIES HERE, FOOD FOR WORMS.

BUT THE WORK SHALL NOT BE WHOLLY LOST:

FOR IT WILL, AS HE BELIEV'D, APPEAR ONCE MORE,

IN A NEW & MORE PERFECT EDITION,

CORRECTED AND AMENDED

BY THE AUTHOR.

HE WAS BORN ON JANUARY 6, 1706.

DIED 17...

It seems a fitting end to an extraordinary tale.

# HORATIO NELSON, 1ST VISCOUNT NELSON

## ADMIRAL AND HERO
### 29 September 1758–21 October 1805
*St Paul's Cathedral Crypt, St Paul's Churchyard,*
*London EC4M 8AD*

We do not know whether we should mourn or rejoice. The
country has gained the most splendid and decisive Victory that
has ever graced the naval annals of England; but it has been
dearly purchased. The great and gallant Nelson is no more.
*The Times*, 6 November 1805

Even now it is thrilling to read about the Battle of
Trafalgar, where Nelson took on the French and Spanish,
his twenty-seven ships to their thirty-three, making the decision to attack in the middle of the night, sending a message
to his fleet: 'England expects that every man will do his
duty.' By 1 p.m. on 21 October 1805 Nelson was shot and by
4.30 p.m. he was dead, having requested that his possessions
be given to Lady Hamilton, his lover and the mother of his
only child, Horatia.

His return to England was, in itself, epic. His body was
placed in a cask of brandy and lashed to the *Victory*'s mainmast.
When the ship reached Gibraltar, the body was transferred to
a lead-lined coffin filled with wine. 'We pickled him!' crowed
the guide at St Paul's Cathedral as he embarked on the story
of Nelson's death and funeral. Rather fittingly, the dispatch
to London about England's greatest naval victory (and the
death of England's greatest admiral) was carried on board
HMS *Pickle*.

It took another month for HMS *Victory* to make it from
Gibraltar to England, where an autopsy was performed (and
the deadly musket ball retrieved). Nelson's body was placed in

another lead coffin filled with brandy. Then, on 21 December, he was placed in another coffin, made of wood from the main mast of *L'Orient*, a French ship destroyed in the Battle of the Nile, which had been given to Nelson years before. This coffin was then placed in another made of lead and then another of wood (I think this is his fifth coffin, if you don't count the first cask, making it the Russian doll of coffins). The multi-coffin was collected from HMS *Victory*, which was moored in the River Medway and taken up the Thames to Greenwich, arriving on 25 December, where it was kept in a private room for another eleven days. It wasn't until 4 January that the coffin was moved to Greenwich Hospital's Painted Hall where he lay in state for three days, with an estimated 100,000 people filing past.

Nelson's body then went, by barge, up the Thames, followed by a two-mile procession of boats, a funeral flotilla the likes of which we have never seen. He was taken to the Admiralty in Whitehall and the funeral was held the next day, 9 January. The funeral procession from Whitehall to St Paul's included royalty, ministers, high-ranking military and 10,000 soldiers. The service was attended by 7,000 people including thirty-two admirals and 100 captains, plus seamen from HMS *Victory*. The service itself ran from 11 a.m. to 6 p.m. when the coffin (how many layers I am not sure) was placed in the black marble sarcophagus that had been originally made for Cardinal Wolsey, who was Lord Chancellor under Henry VIII before falling from favour. His deathbed had remained unused for centuries. Finally, with Nelson, it found someone monumental enough.

It was the grandest of funerals and, today, it remains the grandest of graves. In the magnificent crypt, this sarcopha-gus takes pride of place – even Wellington's tomb, nearby, is plainer – and floats on a mosaic floor with a nautical theme, entwined with dolphins and sea serpents. There is also, above the crypt, in the south quire aisle of St Paul's, a white marble memorial to Nelson, his amputated arm covered by a cloak, as he looks out to what must be the horizon. This was finished in 1818. Down the Strand, in Trafalgar Square, Nelson's Column wasn't finished until 1843. Truly, Nelson as hero is impossible to avoid if you live in London. And yet, set against this, Nelson as man is easy to miss.

There is a huge contrast between his death and that of his beloved mistress. Their relationship, which resulted in their daughter Horatia (I think that name certainly gave the father away) being born 31 January 1801, was the scandal of his age. Nelson left his wife, Fanny, and lived openly with them, much to the upset, not to say fascination, of all. It was his dying wish that they be looked after but, with him now installed as the nation's hero beyond parallel, they were not. Indeed Emma was not even given permission to attend the funeral. The government lavished money and honours on Nelson's brother and family. Emma floundered, falling into catastrophic debt that ended with her and Horatia going to prison, after which they fled to Calais to escape more creditors. Emma died, aged forty-nine, in poverty, in France, a sad end for one of the most famous (or, in her case, infamous) women of her time. Her grave, at the Eglise de St Pierre in Calais, was lost during the First World War.

But what of Horatia? Her life, in comparison to that of her celebrated parents, was decidedly ordinary. But then, by the time she was fifteen, she had lived in prison and run away to France with a woman whom she never really believed was her mother, not least because Emma always insisted she was merely a guardian. After Emma's death, Horatia returned to England, disguised as a boy to escape arrest for her mother's debts in France. But upon arrival at Dover, she was taken in by Nelson's sisters and her life changed completely. She married a neighbour, a clergyman named

Philip Ward, and they lived quietly in rural Norfolk and then Kent, and had ten children.

She ended up in the north-west London suburb of Pinner, of all places, where she had moved after her husband's death to be near her son Nelson. (Another son was named Horatio while a daughter was Horatia.) She is buried in Paines Lane cemetery and I did visit her grave, a raised slab, on a frozen day in December. Her epitaph reads: 'Here lies Horatia Nelson Ward, who died March 6, 1881, aged 80, the beloved daughter of Vice Admiral Lord Nelson and widow of the above named Reverend Philip Ward.' It is quiet here, as it would be, and as far away as possible from the pomp and circumstance of St Paul's.

# POSTMAN'S PARK:
# THE MEMORIAL TO HEROIC SELF-SACRIFICE

**Established 1900**

*City of London, King Edward Street (or St Martin's Le-Grand),*
*London EC1A 7BX*

. Ⅰt was a short and evocative paragraph that ran in *The Times* newspaper on 5 May 1885 about the funeral of Alice Ayres, who had died in a fire in Union Street, Borough. Her coffin, it said, had been carried by sixteen firemen, who relieved each other in sets of four. The service was 'impressive', with twenty girls in white from the village school. 'It had been arranged that these young people should have followed the coffin and sing at the graveside but this was unfortunately prevented by a severe hailstorm.' A large 'assemblage' of people from the village (where she had grown up) attended. The coffin bore the inscription: 'Alice Ayres, died April 26, aged 26'.

This story caught the eye of George Frederic Watts, the celebrated Victorian painter. His portraits had made him rich but this was a man who wore his morality on his smock sleeve, liberally donating his money to good causes and his paintings to galleries that were, themselves, free. His work often highlighted the evils of Mammon and the conditions of the poor. He also was against the killing of birds for their feathers to adorn hats and was president of the Anti-Tight Lacing Society, which, in the age of the wasp waist, when women regularly suffered fainting fits, fought for the right of women to loosen their corsets. But back to Alice Ayres. On 5 September 1887, Mr Watts wrote to *The Times*, his letter appearing under the headline: 'ANOTHER JUBILEE SUGGESTION'. It began:

> Sir – among other ways of commemorating this 50th year of Her Majesty's reign, it would surely be of national interest to

collect a complete record of the stories of heroism in every-day life. The roll would be a long one but I would cite as an example the name of Alice Ayres, the maid of all work at an oil-mongers in Gravel-lane, in April 1885, who lost her life in saving those of her master's children.

He told Alice's story. About how, as flames were seen in the building, a young woman appeared at an upper storey window. The crowd, holding up some clothes to break her fall, entreated her to jump. Instead she went back and re-appeared, dragging a feather bed which she threw out the window. She went away again, this time returning with a child of three in her arms, whom she threw to safety so she landed on the mattress. Twice more she did this with older children. But when her turn came to jump she was too exhausted and, instead of the mattress, landed on the pavement. She was taken to St Thomas' Hospital, where she died.

Mr Watts continues: 'It is not too much to say that the history of Her Majesty's reign would gain a lustre were the nation to erect a monument, say, here in London, to record the names of these likely to be forgotten heroes.' He ended: 'The material prosperity of a nation is not an abiding posses-sion; the deeds of its people are.'

He wanted to build a wall inscribed with the names of his everyday heroes in Hyde Park but it did not happen. He harrumphed that, if he'd proposed a racecourse round the park, then it would have. He and his wife Mary lobbied tirelessly for the project, redrafting their wills to pay for it. But it would take until 1900 for the plan to become real, with Watts paying £700 to build a 50ft-long wooden loggia, with a tiled roof, to house 120 memorial tiles, designed, at first by William De Morgan, in the little green space that is Postman's Park in the City of London. Watts was eighty-three and too ill to attend.

The memorial is still there now, and how the beautiful

tiles fascinate, lined up on the wall, each with its tale to tell. The park itself is one of those marvellous surprises in which London specialises, a manicured jewel of a place, with its trees providing shade and its benches a place to munch a lunch. This is the former burial ground of St Botolph's Aldersgate Church and tombstones are stacked round the edges. But it is the memorial that attracts an endless stream of visitors, many of them tourists, who have come to marvel at ordinary people who died doing extraordinary things.

This is what the tile for Alice Ayres says: 'Daughter of a bricklayer's labourer who by intrepid conduct saved 3 children from a burning house in Union Street Borough at the cost of her own young life. April 24, 1885.' And here is the tile for John Cranmer of Cambridge, aged twenty-three: 'A clerk in the London County Council who was drowned near Ostend whilst saving the life of a stranger and a foreigner.' (I quite like the addition of 'a foreigner', which seems very British.) The names and the tales line up: the stewardess who went down with the sinking ship in 1899, the seventeen-year-old who died trying to save a child from a runaway horse in 1888, the daughter who refused to be deterred from making three attempts to climb a burning staircase to save her aged mum in 1900, the man who saved a 'lunatic woman' from suicide but was himself run over by the train. I looked for a long time at the tile for Sarah Smith, pantomime artiste, who died of injuries received when attempting in her inflammable dress to extinguish the flames which had enveloped her companion.

There is space for 120 tiles but only fifty-three existed when Mary Watts died in 1938. Extraordinarily, in 2007, another tile was added. 'Leigh Pitt, reprographic operator, aged 30, saved a drowning boy from the canal at Thamesmead but sadly was unable to save himself. June 7, 2007.' The Diocese of London has said that it will consider further names to be added. What a good idea.

# THE UNKNOWN WARRIOR

## 1914–1918
*Westminster Abbey, 20 Dean's Yard, London SW1P 3PA*

The ceremony of yesterday was the most beautiful, the most touching, and the most impressive that in all its long, eventful story this island has ever seen…

'The Quick and the Dead', *The Times*, 12 November 1920

The idea for a grave of the Unknown Warrior came from a military padre, the Reverend David Railton, who served in France in 1916. Later he would write about how, one night at dusk, when he had just returned from the line, having laid to rest a fallen comrade, he happened upon a small garden in Erkingham, near Armentières, with a grave. At the head was a rough cross of white wood on which was written, in black pencil: 'An Unknown British Soldier'. 'It was dusk and no one was near, except some officers in the billet playing cards. I remember how still it was. Even the guns seemed to be resting. How that grave caused me to think. Later on, I nearly wrote to [Field Marshal] Sir Douglas Haig to ask if the body of an unknown soldier might be sent home…'

In 1920, now back from France and a vicar in Margate in Kent, Reverend Railton did write that letter, this time addressed to the Dean of Westminster Abbey, who in turn wrote to the government, which agreed. Thus, on the night of 7 November, four bodies were exhumed from the four main battle areas in France: the Aisne, the Somme, Ypres and Arras. They were brought to the chapel at St Pol, each wrapped in a Union Jack. The officer in charge pointed to one. The others were reburied.

The next day the body began a journey, taken first to Boulogne and placed in a coffin of English oak. On

9 November, British troops took over guard duties from the French and the body crossed the Channel on the destroyer *Verdun*. It arrived at Dover to a 19-gun salute and began making its way, by train, to London. This is what the *Mail* wrote: 'The train thundered through the dark, wet, moonless night. At the platforms by which it rushed could be seen groups of women watching and silent, many dressed in deep mourning.' On the morning of 11 November, the body was put on a gun carriage, pulled by six black horses, the procession watched in silence by what *The Times*, in its report, called a multitude. 'Pity for this plain man who had done his full duty, more than once filled the eyes of the onlookers with tears – an outbreak of emotion very rare with English crowds.'

The King was the chief mourner, the twelve pall-bearers captains of land, while sea and air and 100 VCs provided the guard of honour. 'Such a guard as no monarch ever had,' notes the paper's report. The body was buried in earth brought from a French battlefield. The burial service, in the abbey, was spoken over one body that was, in fact, everybody who had died in the Great War. 'Those who heard them felt that they were uttered also for all the hundreds of thousands, his comrades in death as in life, who rest in far-off graves from Flanders to Mesopotamia, or who sleep their last sleep beneath our guardian seas.' The last words were Kipling's *Recessional* which includes the refrain: 'Lest we forget – Lest we forget!'

When I visited Westminster Abbey, I did not know which grave I would choose. I wanted to find one special one and I had thought it might be Charles Darwin, though, as I walked by the statue of William Wilberforce, with its novella of an inscription, I was tempted to pick him. Then there was Handel, looking rather camp it must be said, with his *Messiah*. More than 3,000 people are buried in the abbey, including five kings and four queens, and there are 600 tombs and monuments.

So many fine words about the great and the good that you could spend all day reading them. But it was the grave of the Unknown Warrior that moved me – its simple black floor-slab, surrounded by poppies and, when I visited, adorned by two wreaths from the Korean embassy. Every official state visit starts here. On the pillars nearby are Reverend Railton's flag, which had covered the coffin on its final journey, and a bell from HMS *Verdun*. On the grave it says: 'They buried him among the kings because he had done good towards God and towards his house.' This, out of all the 3,000, is the most famous grave here.

# ATHENA

## OWLET
### 5 June 1850–1855
*Florence Nightingale Museum, St Thomas' Hospital, Westminster Bridge Road, London SE1 7EH*

For her story, see the entry for Florence Nightingale in South-West England.

*Karl Marx, Highgate Cemetery*

# LONDON: NORTH AND WEST OF THE THAMES

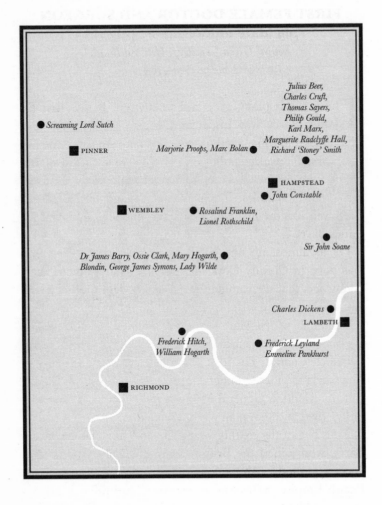

Screaming Lord Sutch

PINNER

Marjorie Proops, Marc Bolan

Julius Beer,
Charles Cruft,
Thomas Sayers,
Philip Gould,
Karl Marx,
Marguerite Radclyffe Hall,
Richard 'Stoney' Smith

HAMPSTEAD

John Constable

WEMBLEY

Rosalind Franklin,
Lionel Rothschild

Sir John Soane

Dr James Barry, Ossie Clark, Mary Hogarth,
Blondin, George James Symons, Lady Wilde

Charles Dickens

LAMBETH

Frederick Hitch,
William Hogarth

Frederick Leyland
Emmeline Pankhurst

RICHMOND

# DR JAMES BARRY (BORN MARGARET ANN BULKLEY)

## FIRST FEMALE DOCTOR AND SURGEON
### 1799 (date unknown)–25 July 1865
*Kensal Green Cemetery, Harrow Road,*
*London W10 4RA*

The grave is plain, grey and weathered. It says that Dr James Barry was Inspector General of Hospitals and that he died in 1865, aged seventy. But beneath this stone lies the body of a woman who hid her true sex for most of her life in order to pursue a medical career that was, at the time, forbidden to females. It is generally thought Dr Elizabeth Blackwell was the first woman doctor, but actually it was Dr James Barry.

Or, as almost no one knew, Margaret Ann Bulkley. She was born in County Cork in Ireland and announced, at a young age, that she wanted to be a doctor. Her mother Mary Anne, who was the sister of the artist James Barry, cooked up a scheme in which Margaret, aged fourteen, would enrol at the School of Medicine at the University of Edinburgh, using her uncle's name. The idea was that s/he would then go to Venezuela to practise under the protection of a family friend. But the friend, a General Miranda (no relation to Carmen, sadly), died and that plan was scuppered.

Thus began the extraordinary life and times of Dr James Barry, who joined the British Army medical corps in 1813 and was posted to Africa, followed by other stints around the British Empire. S/he was an eccentric and difficult person but, crucially, an exceptional surgeon, performing the first successful Caesarean section in 1826. S/he was an outspoken, not to say bombastic, campaigner of hospital sanitation who took on the likes of Florence Nightingale in Crimea (who pronounced her/him 'a brute'). Still, it was Dr Barry's hospital that had the best mortality record.

It is often said that a woman in a man's world has to be twice as good and Dr Barry may prove the point. But s/he was also, by all accounts, and I am indebted for these details in particular to Mike Rendell, an aficionado of the period who is fascinated by this story, an oddball. Dr Barry was deeply attached to a large black poodle named Psyche and also kept a goat, in order to drink the milk. She was a tee-totaller but did advocate bathing in wine. Early on, she found a Jamaican manservant named John who, we must assume, knew everything and helped her to hide her secret.

How did she do this? How do you hide the fact that you are a woman when you are only 5ft tall and have a high-pitched voice? Dr Barry wore lifts in her shoes and used towels to pad out her body, especially her shoulders. S/he was cantankerous and challenged anyone who doubted her masculinity to a duel and, indeed, did shoot someone. She developed a reputation as a ladies' man (although, early on in her career, she was investigated for having an 'unnaturally close' relationship to a man). Her temper was as fiery as her hair and she was court-martialled on several occasions. But, always, incredibly, she bounced back and she retired, after serving finally in Canada, in 1857, having achieved the rank of Inspector General of Hospitals.

Dr Barry had left instructions that no post-mortem should be carried out but the body still had to be prepared for burial. This was done by a charwoman named Sophia Bishop who didn't take long to spot the difference. It wasn't until after the funeral, though, that she told the doctor who had declared Dr Barry 'male' on the death certificate that *he* was, in fact, a *she* and indeed, from the stretch marks in her abdomen, had had a baby (this may have been a result of the 'unnaturally close' relationship). The doctor promptly wrote a letter protesting that he had always thought that Dr Barry may have been a hermaphrodite. The Army, appalled that such a successful surgeon had managed to hide her sex for forty-six years, sealed the records for a century. It wasn't until 2008 that letters unearthed by historians finally settled the mystery for good. Still, the gravestone, in square 67 of the cemetery map, row 6, hasn't been touched. The masquerade of Dr James Barry continues in death, as it did in life.

## JULIUS BEER

**FINANCIER**
**30 September 1836–28 February 1880**
*Beer Mausoleum, Highgate Cemetery (West),*
*Swains Lane, London N6 6PJ*

## RACHEL BEER (NÉE SASSOON)

**EDITOR AND WRITER**
**7 April 1858–29 April 1927**
*Kent and Sussex Cemetery, Benhall Mill Road,*
*Royal Tunbridge Wells TN2 5JJ*

At the highest point in Highgate Cemetery stands a fantastical structure that is the family mausoleum of Julius Beer, a Jewish immigrant from Frankfurt who, in 1854, at the age of eighteen, arrived in England with nothing. A wheeler and dealer or, as they say, financier, he set out to become rich and incorporate himself into English society – something he accomplished with impressive alacrity, the process very much facilitated by marrying an English Anglican with the extraordinary name of Thyrza Keren-Happuch. The Beers were the definition of nouveau riche – touring the world, deal-making, accumulating all manner of objects (and *objets*) including, in 1870, the *Observer* newspaper. And so, when tragedy struck and their daughter Ada died at the age of eight, Julius decided nothing would do but to have her incarcerated in splendour in Highgate Cemetery.

What happened after this is a morality tale. Julius Beer bought his plot for £800 in 1876 and asked Sir George Gilbert Scott, who had just completed the Albert Memorial, to help. In the end, Sir George's son John designed the 50ft-high Portland stone and marble edifice, with a pyramid roof and stained glass dome. Inside, blue and gold mosaics from Italy were laid by Giulio Salviati, who had also worked on the Albert Memorial. It cost £5,000, a fortune in those days. Sir Nikolaus Pevsner described the roof as 'à la Halicarnassus', which made everyone think that Julius Beer had sought to emulate the Seven Wonders of the World. The artist Henry Hugh Armstead, who had made the eighty-four life-sized figures in marble for the podium on the Albert Memorial (a theme is emerging here, you will notice), was approached to carve the marble relief of an angel embracing a girl, whose face was said to be based on Ada's death mask. It was called *Memorial to My Only Daughter*. The fact that Julius Beer was a Jew, if one who had had his children baptised, seemed to have been overlooked by the cemetery.

Our tale now skips a generation. Julius died in 1880 and was duly interred in his tomb mansion. In 1887 his son and heir, the now fantastically rich Frederick, married Rachel Sassoon, born in Bombay to the famed Jewish family, originally from Baghdad (and then India), but now very much at home in England. It was a love match and the couple had a church wedding, something that Rachel's family never forgave her for, though it was attended by none other than William Gladstone

(who was in between prime ministerships). Their lives were quite extraordinary, as chronicled by their biographers in *The First Lady of Fleet Street*, their Mayfair mansion lavishly furnished, their lives the definition of pomp and circumstance. Rachel began to write for *The Observer*, becoming an assistant editor, astonishing in an age when women were very firmly second-class citizens. She enjoyed it so much that, in 1893, Frederick bought her the *Sunday Times* to edit. Her interests and writings ranged far and wide, and included in particular foreign affairs and British politics. Her role in the Dreyfus Affair was crucial. Reading about it now, it all seems quite the fairy tale starring a heroine way ahead of her time.

But then something happened. Frederick died in 1901, the gates of the Beer Mausoleum opening for the first time in decades for his coffin. Rachel, finding herself alone, most of her family having abandoned her over her marriage, fell apart. She took refuge with her sister-in-law in Tunbridge Wells. Her grief was overwhelming and persistent (not unlike Queen Victoria's, her biographers note). In addition to her erratic behaviour there was the irrefutable fact that she was, for the times in which she lived, just plain odd: a childless career woman in a man's world who spent most of her time reading and writing. Her family had her examined for insanity by various doctors and in 1903 the Master of Lunacy visited and pronounced her as a person of unsound mind.

She spent the next twenty years, until her death in 1927, living in a Tunbridge Wells mansion with three mental health nurses for company. As a lunatic, she was not allowed to make a will. She would have wanted to be interred next to Frederick. Her nephews, who included the poet Siegfried, were her heirs. They now decided her final fate, rejecting the fabulous mausoleum for the unconsecrated section (her acquired Anglican-ness now forgotten) of the Tunbridge Wells municipal cemetery (now called the Kent and Sussex Cemetery). It's a small and ordinary grave, extraordinary only for what it does not say. Her erasure as an independent woman was made complete by the headstone on which she is identified only as 'Daughter of the late David Sassoon'. No birth date. No mention of Frederick. Or the fact that she was the first female newspaper editor in Britain. Her passing merited no mention in the *Sunday Times* and a few fleeting phrases in *The Observer*.

But what of that great mausoleum, which now had no family to look after it? Abandoned and decaying, the former wonder of the world had, by the 1950s, become a pigeon slum, the floor deep in guano. Visitors to Highgate had no idea who Julius Beer was. Was he something to do with diamonds as in De Beers? Writer Alan Brien, visiting it then, commented: 'Julius Beer, whoever he was, has raised for himself a bird Belsen, a privy for pigeons, all his money has turned to a tower of excreta.' The building inspired the Scottish poet Edwin Morgan, but not in a good way: 'In the diamondman's invisible bones / nothing takes root but death'. Eventually, in 1975, the Friends of Highgate Cemetery moved in to start the big clean up. The mountain of guano meant the iron gates could not be opened. Cleaners, wearing masks, had to be lowered down from a window. The lower part of the mausoleum had been used as a storeroom. The coffins of the Beer family were found broken open and empty.

It is gleaming and beautiful now, if you like that sort of thing. English Heritage spent £42,000 in 1993 to restore it to its full glory. The pigeons are long gone, the mosaic restored and the gold glistening. But should you pay a visit to this extravagant foray into attempted immortality, cast a thought to that other grave in Tunbridge Wells, simple and barren of detail, occupied by a remarkable woman, the first female to edit a newspaper in Britain, who was destroyed by the times in which she lived.

## MARC BOLAN (FELD)

### ROCK STAR
#### 30 September 1947–16 September 1977
*Golders Green Crematorium, Hoop Lane, London NW11 7NL*

To say that Marc Bolan, the curly haired, purple-satined, feather boa'd star of glam rock band T-Rex, has become a myth is to do down the idea of myths. Sometimes, when I look at the sheer number of tributes and shrines, and the amount of energy devoted to him, I think that even Icarus has been outdone. But then Icarus only had wings constructed by feathers and wax. Marc Bolan had his very own white swan to ride. I refer, of course, to his first Tyrannosaurus Rex hit, 'Ride a White Swan', a short, simple, catchy number that includes the marvellous last line 'Wear your hair long, babe you can't go wrong.' The song was only stopped from reaching the top of the UK Top 40 in 1970 by a novelty record from *Dad's Army* actor Clive Dunn called 'Granddad'.

Even now it is impossible not to listen to 'Ride a White Swan' without starting to bop along. He may have been born Mark Feld, the son of a lorry driver from Hackney, but he found his destiny as a rock star named Bolan: sexy, good-looking, charismatic, a character who caught the zeitgeist, probably by lassoing it with a feather boa. But, in death, which came two weeks before his 30th birthday, he was even more famous. The sycamore tree in Gipsy Lane in Barnes in south-west London, into which the purple Mini he was travelling in from a club in Berkeley Square crashed, is now a shrine of shrines. In tourist guides, it regularly gets four stars (though surely, for Bolan, a whole sky-full is needed). It is described as a 'must visit' for 1970s rock fans and features a bronze bust which was unveiled by his son Rolan Bolan in 2002. It is recognised by the English Tourist Board as a site of rock 'n' roll importance, which is so strange on so many levels that I had to mention it.

At his funeral, his devastated parents said that fans were welcome to come and so they did. The news reports now look grainy and jerky but they are also undeniably glamorous. There was David Bowie in his trilby and his shades getting out of a limo. There were Rod Stewart and (of course) blondes. The legendary Les Paul and Eric Clapton were there. There were journalists too. The service, by a rabbi, was private. Among the many floral tributes was a gigantic swan fashioned from white chrysanthemums, from Marc's manager Tony Howard.

The swan is still very much in evidence at Golders Green Crematorium and garden which, by the way, has a markedly peaceful atmosphere. When I went in search of his family rose-bush (West Rosebed, Section 5, Plot E, 35979), I found a little china swan underneath it. And, in the square brick entrance-way, on what I call the Wall of Fame, he has two plaques. The first is his main memorial and he is up there ('Musician, writer and poet') next to The Who drummer Keith Moon, who died in 1978 ('There is no substitute') and not far from Ronnie Scott, who died in 1996 ('Jazz musician, club proprie-tor, raconteur and wit'). There is also another plaque, shiny black granite with gold lettering and an etching of Bolan with that amazing hair. This was placed by the Official Marc Bolan Fan Club on the 25th anniversary of his death. Underneath, on the ledge, someone has placed a white china swan. And, just to complete the flock, there is also a bench, the back of which is a swan in flight, put in place on the 35th anniversary of his death, which is opposite the rosebed.

But surely, for Marc, you can never have too many swans. I quite like this quote from Marc Almond of Soft Cell: 'He was the winner in the end. Maybe he had to die young for that to happen. But it would be great if he could look down from somewhere and know that he is still a star – and always will been.' To be honest, my only regret is that when I visited it was raining and I was wearing flowered wellies and a beret. Surely it would have been far better to be in purple satin with a boa or two flowing behind me.

# RAYMOND 'OSSIE' CLARK

## FASHION DESIGNER
### 9 June 1942–6 August 1996
*Kensal Green Cemetery, Harrow Road, London W10 4RA*

It feels as if Ossie Clark, the legendary sixties icon, is everywhere now. His clothes adorn models in the new V&A fashion rooms, the David Hockney portrait of him and his wife Celia Birtwell and his cat Percy hangs in the Tate Britain, and he can be seen in the form of his lovely slinky and sexy creations on the bodies of Kate Moss and others. It was not always thus. Ossie Clark, a working-class boy whose nickname came from the village he was born in, Oswaldtwistle in Lancashire, was the classic case of a man who flew too close to the sun.

Now, with hindsight, he is spoken of as the man who could have been our Yves Saint Laurent but who never found his financial backer. But what he surely was, without compare, was swinging sixties London. Drugs, sex and rock 'n' roll didn't seem like a cliché then, though in his case, because of his clothes and his skill at 'cutting' to fit the female form, that would have to be modified to be drugs, sexiness and rock 'n' roll. Film-maker Derek Jarman, when he first met Ossie at the Slade School of Art in London in 1963, wrote: 'Decadence, I learnt, was the first sign of intelligence.' Apparently, Ossie Clark was the man responsible for the motorcycle jacket, hot pants and maxi coats. Imagine a world without those. He gave Mick Jagger the jumpsuit. Imagine a world without that! At his shows The Beatles would be in the front row, with Patti Boyd, George Harrison's girlfriend, modelling.

It all went wrong relatively early on. He was divorced in 1975 and bankrupt by 1983. Drugs and drink certainly played a part in his spectacular fall from grace. It all ended in a chaotic West London council flat in 1996 when he was stabbed by a former lover, Diego Cogalata, who went to prison for the killing. In the days afterwards, the newspapers poured over his story and one recalled that in 1994, in a 'correspondent's question' in the *Daily Mail*, a reader had written in asking, 'Whatever happened to Ossie Clark?' Ossie himself wrote back to say that in the mid-1980s he'd lost his love of fashion. 'I had the same ups and downs most people have, but I enjoyed the next ten years and felt privileged at being my own master. I feel this is the most important thing for a creative mind, even if it causes financial hardship,' he noted, adding, 'I've decided I'm ready to return to designing. I've had discussions about setting up my own studio, and I'm waiting for offers from potential patrons.' It never happened but he resides now in square 162 at Kensal Green, in some splendour, with an elegant tall slate gravestone that, with its flowing symbols and handwriting, seems positively groovy. But then he may have almost invented that.

# CHARLES ALFRED CRUFT

## DOG SHOW PROMOTER
### 28 June 1852–10 September 1938
*Highgate Cemetery (West) Swains Lane, London N6 6PJ*

# THOMAS SAYERS

## PUGILIST
### 25 May 1826–8 November 1865
*Highgate Cemetery (West), as above*

This is a tale that wags the dog. When I was trundling through Highgate Cemetery, on the wild western side, two graves struck me as being related. The first was that of Charles Cruft, the man who founded the most famous dog show in the world. His tomb, though substantial and, of course, in Highgate, which befits a man of his standing, is just a bit dull, a rectangular multi-layered slab with his name on it. Practical and no-nonsense, this grave has not even a yip of soul or romance. But then Mr Cruft was, first and foremost, a businessman. When he saw a dog, he saw money. His obituary in *The Times* described him as 'founder of the dog show', not as a dog lover. He was the son of a jeweller who began his working life as a clerk at Spratt's dog biscuit company, eventually rising to general manager, and virtually inventing what we now know as dry dog food. He encouraged canine clubs and societies, as pedigrees would lead to better feeding (and, not incidentally, dog biscuit sales). For his shows, he began in 1886 with terriers (appropriate, given his tenacity). By 1914, having persuaded members of the royal family to compete, his was a name already known around the world.

There is no doubt that Charles Cruft was dogged but did

he love dogs? Indeed, did he even own dogs? His second wife, Emma, said in *Mrs Charles Cruft's Famous Dog Book* (published 1949) that they feared that, by owning a dog, they would be seen as favouring one breed, which would of course be bad for business. 'We were determined to own a pet, so we took the least line of resistance and kept – a CAT!' In Charles Cruft's own memoir, published posthumously, he claimed that he and Emma had owned a St Bernard, the breed that appears on the Crufts logo but not, of course, on the grave.

But nearby there is a grave that seems as if it should be his, as it is guarded by a magnificent canine, a mastiff, eyes open, watchful and sad. This was a dog called Lion and the man inside the tomb is Thomas Sayers, the great bare-knuckle prize-fighter. Tom, as he was called, was born poor, in Brighton, could hardly write and was barely educated, lived a chaotic life, unlucky in love, a bricklayer by trade. He wasn't a big man – 5ft 8½in. tall, weighing about 155lbs – but he could fight. Prize-fighting was illegal but that doesn't seem to have hindered it much. It's all rather mythical now but Tom fought – and won – against much larger men. Indeed, he became British Heavyweight Champion (how this was possible when it was illegal, I don't know). Of sixteen fights, Tom, the Brighton Titch, described by the papers as the 'small clever little ring general', lost only one.

His last fight was the most famous: the first and supposedly the best 'fight of the century', and certainly the first World Heavyweight Championship, against American John Carmel Heenan or, as reporters at the time referred to him, Hercules. He was forty pounds heavier, five inches taller and eight years younger than Sayer. The fight (still illegal, remember) became an obsessive talking point on both sides of the Atlantic. As *Harper's Weekly* put it: 'The bulk of the people in England and America are heart and soul engrossed in a fight compared to which a Spanish bull-bait is but a mild and diverting pastime.'

It took place on 17 April 1860 at 7.30 a.m. in a field in Farnborough, Hampshire. In attendance were some 12,000 people including the nineteen-year-old Prince of Wales, Charles Dickens (of course, for he seems to be everywhere) and the Prime Minister, Lord Palmerston. It was a ferocious battle, lasting two hours and twenty minutes or forty-two rounds. Bloody and battered, they did not finish until the ring was stormed by the Aldershot police. This is the scene, as described by a reporter from *Bell's Life*: 'The final round was merely a wild scramble, both men ordered to desist from fighting. The Blues being now in force, there was, of course, no chance of the men continuing, and adjournment was necessary. Heenan had rushed away from the ring, and ran some distance with the activity of a deer, and although he was as fit as ever, he was obviously totally blind. Sayers, although tired, was also strong on his pins and could have fought some time longer, although by then the authorities were up in arms in all directions, so it would be a mere waste of time to go elsewhere.' It wasn't long before Palmerston was being asked questions in the Commons and, by 1865, the Queensberry Rules would be in place.

But back to our tale. Sayers never fought again. He escaped arrest and retired to drink champagne at The Swan on the Old Kent Road. The public raised an incredible £3,000 for him to live the good life, which is what he did. He was universally adored and hobnobbed with all levels of society. His best friend and constant companion was his mastiff Lion, given to him by Lord Derby, a fan. He and Lion were the toast (literally) of London, and this was probably his undoing. Within five years of the fight, Sayers would be dead at the age of thirty-nine. Tens of thousands (accounts differ from 10,000 to 100,000) came to his funeral at Highgate where Lion, who would outlive him by three years, was chief mourner.

Charles Cruft would have been eight when the 'Fight of

the Century' took place. Did he know about it? He would
have been thirteen, just about to begin his career as a dog
biscuit impresario, when Tom Sayers died. Did he know
about the funeral or even possibly attend? In later life did
he ever wander around Highgate, and see Lion's mournful
eyes? When I first saw these graves, I thought they had gotten
mixed up but that is, of course, fanciful. Still, in some way,
they really are related.

# CHARLES JOHN HUFFAM DICKENS

## WRITER
### 7 February 1812–9 June 1870
*Westminster Abbey, 20 Dean's Yard London SW1P 3PA*


# MARY SCOTT HOGARTH

## SISTER AND MUSE
### 26 October 1819–7 May 1837
*Kensal Green Cemetery, Harrow Road, London W10 4RA*


There aren't many novels that have a cemetery as their lead character, but then *Her Fearful Symmetry* by Audrey Niffenegger is a very special book. It is, in many ways, a love letter to Highgate Cemetery. One of her other (human) main characters, Robert, is a guide at the cemetery and here he is, giving one of his tours, explaining why, by 1850, overcrowded churchyards were a health hazard. 'If you've read your Dickens, you know what I'm talking about: elbows poking out of the ground, grave robbers stealing the dead to sell them to medical schools. It was an absolute shambles.'

Well I have to say that I feel the same about Dickens. At times it seemed as if every graveyard that I visited has some bit of the great man, ego-maniac and hyperactive genius that he was, poking up out of the ground in one way or another. Indeed, he is linked to at least eight of the graves in this book, either by his books, his journalism or, in this case, his family. It is fitting that his estranged wife Catherine is buried at Highgate itself, for it was the absolute place to be seen dead in Victorian England, and Catherine, ever worried about her status, would have had nothing less.

But the only possible place to start the Dickens graveyard

trail is further west, at Kensal Green. 'We have seventy-one graves here connected to Dickens,' said one of the guides. Seventy-one! Most of these are his friends and acquaintances (including fellow novelist Wilkie Collins). By far the most important is his sister-in-law, Mary Hogarth, whom Dickens adored to the point of obsession. She died at the age of seventeen, in his arms, probably of heart failure or a stroke. Charles, who was only twenty-five, took a ring from her fingers and wore it for the rest of his life. A small industry has been devoted to explaining the intense influence that her death had on Dickens. It does seem that the man was simply unhinged by her. This, for instance, is what he wrote to his close friend, Tom Beard: 'Thank God she died in my arms and that the very last words she whispered were of me ... I solemnly believe that so perfect a creature never breathed. I knew her inmost heart and her real worth and value. She had not a fault...'

Dickens claimed that Mary was 'the spirit which directs my life'. He certainly was the spirit who directed her funeral, paying for her grave and composing the epitaph:

MARY SCOTT HOGARTH. DIED 7TH MAY 1837. YOUNG, BEAUTIFUL
AND GOOD, GOD IN HIS MERCY NUMBERED HER WITH HIS ANGELS
AT THE EARLY AGE OF SEVENTEEN.

It was his intention to be buried in the same grave (by the path in square 33 of the cemetery) and he was most put out when her brother George died in 1841. 'It is a great trial for me to give up Mary's grave,' wrote Dickens to a friend. 'The desire to be buried next to her is as strong upon me now, as it was five years ago ... And I KNOW that it will never diminish. I cannot bear the thought of being excluded from her dust.' But, in the end, George was buried with his sister.

The next death was of Dickens himself in 1870 at his

house, Gad's Hill, near Rochester in Kent. He had been estranged from his wife since 1858 when Catherine had accidently received a bracelet intended for his mistress, the actress Ellen Ternan. Of course, the man who had written so much about funerals in his novels had micro-managed his own: 'I emphatically direct that I be buried in an inexpensive, unostentatious and strictly private manner; that no public announcement be made of the time or place of my burial; that at the utmost not more than three plain mourning coaches be employed; and that those who attend my funeral wear no scarf, cloak, black bow, long hat-band or other such revolting absurdity.' Apparently Dickens had wanted to be buried in or near Rochester but *The Times* newspaper had other ideas, campaigning for him to be buried in Westminster Abbey. *The Times* won, though surely if Dickens really hadn't wanted to be there, he would have said so.

The funeral operation was carried out like some sort of secret spy mission. The grave in Poets' Corner was dug during the night of 13 June. The next morning the body was carried to London by train and then in an anonymous hearse, arriving at the abbey at 9.30 a.m. Only twelve people, family and friends, attended the service, held in the almost empty and silent abbey. Dickens had (of course) decreed what his tombstone would say: the man of so many words wanted none of them on his tombstone. His name should be 'inscribed in plain English letters'. And so it was but, with journalists clamouring at the abbey doors, it was agreed that the grave should be left open for two days and thus, in the end, thousands of people came to pay their respects, throwing in flowers. It was a scene that could have been written by the great man himself.

*The Times* lists all the occupants of the (three) funeral carriages and it is no surprise that they did not include his estranged wife Catherine, who had been blamed by her

husband for all manners of things including, apparently, the
birth of their ten children. One of them, Nora, who died in
infancy, is buried with her in Highgate. Thus while Kensal
Green seems to contain all the drama, not to mention the fun,
Highgate has the blood. Also in the cemetery are Dickens's
parents, the famously indebted John and Elizabeth, his sister
Fanny and his younger brother Alfred. There is nothing
dramatic about these Highgate graves but when you've lived
lives such as they have, perhaps it is best to be boring in death.
(Ideally I would have included these on my graves list but
they are hard to access, as they are not featured in the regular
tour of the western half of Highgate.) Indeed the whole saga
of the Dickens graves – not least the fact that the man who
wanted no fuss at his ended up in the most famous resting
place in all of England – could be a novel in itself except, of
course, that the author who could write it best is dead.

# ROSALIND ELSIE FRANKLIN

## SCIENTIST
### 25 July 1920–16 April 1958
*Willesden United Synagogue Cemetery, Beaconsfield Road,*
*London NW10 2JE*

I do not get the impression that Rosalind Franklin would have indulged much in the 'what if' game. She was a logical and precise woman, who loved facts. But as you look down on her grave, a plain white marble slab, the word 'SCIENTIST' shouting out its pride, it is hard not to wonder 'what if?' First, what if she hadn't died so young, from ovarian cancer at the age of thirty-seven? Would she, eventually, have received the credit she deserved in the discovery of the structure of DNA? Would she, in 1962, alongside Francis Crick, James Watson and Maurice Wilkins, have been awarded the Nobel Prize? And, if that had happened, what else would she have done in her brilliant career?

Of course we will never know – speculation being the enemy of fact – but it is the question that hangs over her still. Rosalind knew, from the age of fifteen, exactly what she wanted to be – a SCIENTIST. Her father, apparently, thought not. She went to Cambridge in 1938 to study physical chemistry, despite her father's views, and got her BA in 1941. She began working on coal and the structure of graphite, receiving her PhD in 1945. After the war, she went to Paris to work and developed an expertise in X-ray crystallography.

When she returned to London, to King's College, she was asked to work on DNA and began to take X-ray diffraction photographs of the beautiful double-stranded chain. Maurice Wilkins was at the same laboratory but, due to the kind of messy mistakes in communication that logic and reason never allow for, they didn't work together. Indeed, there seems to have been zero cooperation, which, as they were in the same lab, tells you something. Meanwhile, over at the Cavendish Laboratory in Cambridge, Crick and Watson were beavering away: at one point, Wilkins showed them one of Franklin's X-ray photographs (unbeknownst to her) which, for them, provided the last piece of evidence confirming the double-helix structure. Her direct link to the discovery was never acknowledged. By all accounts her time at male-dominated King's, where, for instance, women were not allowed in the dining room, wasn't the happiest. Her sister's biography, *My Sister Rosalind Franklin*, covers it in a chapter entitled 'Misery in London'.

The race to discover DNA has become the stuff of legend, that rarest of things, a gripping story involving laboratories. One of the oddities is that all of this would have been one of those facts lost in the midst of time had it not been for Watson's 1968 memoir, *The Double Helix*, in which Franklin was characterised as 'Rosy', a bad-tempered and arrogant type who refused to share her research with colleagues. This characterisation sparked protest and resulted in a counter-biography which was followed in 2002 by Brenda Maddox's biography, *The Dark Lady of DNA*.

Rosalind would know none of this. Indeed, before Crick and Watson had published their findings in 1953, she had turned her attention to the structure of plant viruses, again using X-ray diffraction. Her epitaph says: 'Her research and discoveries on viruses remain of lasting benefit to mankind.' There are those who would make the dark lady of DNA a feminist martyr, a woman cheated out of her place in history. But there are no facts to support the idea that she would share this view. Indeed her sister, in her book, concentrates on her other highly successful research areas.

I must admit that I had no idea that Rosalind Franklin existed until I went to Willesden (this is an Orthodox Jewish cemetery so men must wear hats and women need to cover their shoulders) to see the Rothschild graves. It was Alfred, one of the cemetery caretakers, who told me about her, taking me over to Section N to see the grave. 'She is our most visited grave,' he says. 'There were people here this morning, from America I think.' There are many famous people in this cemetery but Rosalind Franklin is the one they come to visit. Now that tells you something.

# PHILIP GOULD, BARON GOULD
# OF BROOKWOOD

## POLITICAL STRATEGIST
### 30 March 1950–6 November 2011
*Highgate Cemetery (East), Swains Lane, London N6 6PJ*

As you enter the eastern gates, the tamer side of this wild and beautiful cemetery, you walk onto a path that I call the Highgate Walk of Fame. There, on the right, isn't that the Foyles of bookshop fame? And look at that beautiful figure on sculptor Anna Mahler's grave! And, there, on the left, is a big fat pot of pens, placed there in tribute to Douglas Adams, the man who gave us *The Hitchhiker's Guide to the Galaxy*. I note that, in the cemetery's guide to graves of 'notables', he is number one and not, as I would have expected, forty-two, which he identified as the answer to life, the universe and everything. And there, on the left, right in the middle of it all, where he loved to be, is a tall and graceful monument to Philip Gould, the Labour political obsessive and author who died at age sixty-one from throat cancer.

'Labour peer and strategist', says his epitaph. For some, 'strategist' may not sound grand but, in politics, you are nothing without strategy. Philip Gould did not invent New Labour but, without him, it would not have been what it was. His polling and focus groups, not to mention his incredible drive, reinvigorated politics in the 1990s. He loved politics in a way that few do, not for ego or ideology or personal benefit, but because he believed it could change the world. In a world of plastic politicians, where you often find yourself confronted with a really quite weird mixture of power and pastiche, Philip Gould was the real deal and you knew it the moment you met him.

I did that only once, interviewing him for a radio piece

for the BBC, in his grand and airy front room, which was a riot of colour, overlooking Regent's Park. I was struck immediately by his passion, a much over-used word but, in this case, accurate. As he described how, after Labour's traumatic defeat in 1992, he had travelled to visit Bill Clinton's first presidential campaign in Arkansas, it was cinematic. I looked at the producer and we both prayed that the tape recorders were working.

> So I sort of got on a plane and flew to Little Rock and I kind of just arrived and I remember this extraordinarily hazy, hot evening and there were these guys playing kind of pool or something under a tree, and the whole thing was like the South. And I went into this campaigning headquarter and it was like entering an entirely different world. I mean the place was just alive with energy and hope and optimism and enthusiasm in quite the most *remarkable* way. It was like leaving the land of the dead and arriving in the land of the living. And honestly the first thing anyone said to me is, 'Ah, you're Philip Gould. Ah, you've just lost.' And I said 'Yes' and I felt really, really low and rather ashamed to be there. And they said, 'Look, you know in our world losing is the first step to winning', and you know that was their whole attitude.

That trip would end up changing our elections too.

> The truth is they invented in Little Rock an entirely different sort of campaigning based around collegiateness, openness, lack of hierarchy, a kind of flat management structure, and, of course, the War Room which meant there was one place where all the information flowed in and out, all the decisions were made, rapid response, message, the discipline of message. All the modern rules of campaigning were developed there and I call that Total Campaigning and I was there. We

reconstructed in Milbank a kind of Little Rock Clinton model.
And so you know campaigning had changed at a stroke.

Can you hear the romance? Few have the ability to describe
the political world in that way. I suppose it was natural for
him, then, to treat his battle with oesophageal cancer, diagnosed in 2008, as if it were a political battle. He wrote about
this in his book *When I Die: Lessons from the Death Zone*.

> Everything I thought about the battle with cancer was stra-
> tegic, as if I were fighting an election campaign. I saw the
> elimination of the cancer as victory and the test results as
> opinion polls. People might have thought I was mad, and
> in a way I probably was, but that was how I felt, how I had
> always lived my life. I loved politics and loved elections even
> more … Above all I loved to think, to strategise, to solve the
> unanswerable political problem. And this is what I was doing
> now, thinking constantly, not just about how to get through but
> about the best way of getting through.

He died in 2011 and his book, published posthumously,
deals with death head-on: he blows away the cobwebs, the
secrecy, the squeamishness. He describes how he chose his
own gravesite, after his phone call to Highgate Cemetery was
answered by a man named Victor who identified himself as
the chief gravedigger. 'Of course I expected Victor to be a six-
foot-six giant with a big shovel over one shoulder. And when I
met him he turned out to be a six-foot-six giant with a shovel
over one shoulder.' Philip and his wife Gail walk around the
cemetery but nothing catches his eye. 'I wanted a bigger plot,
somewhere that could become almost a communal place for
our family and friends. I was looking not so much for a burial
plot as a burial place, I suppose, a meeting place, something
physical that you could see and connect to.' Eventually, they

find *the* spot, just back from the path, on my Walk of Fame. Philip Gould knew that people, and not just those who knew him, would look up and see his monument, perhaps appreciating the flowers (pansies when I was last there). 'There will be people about the place looking at the graves, looking at my grave, so it will be almost a communal meeting point between the dead and the living. It sounds very romantic, I know. But the dead and the living are both part of our lives. It gives me great comfort to know that I will be there.'

Lord Gould, while he was dying, was photographed at his own grave. It's the kind of thing that may not catch on but it gave him comfort. And so here too he will have the last word: 'This morning I stood at my grave and I thought: God, I do feel very very happy to be going to this place. That is a small victory for a different view of death.'

# JEAN FRANÇOIS GRAVELET ('BLONDIN')

## ENTERTAINER
### 28 February 1824–22 February 1897
*Kensal Green Cemetery, Harrow Road, London W10 4RA*

'Funambulist isn't a word you hear every day though surely it should be, for it means tightrope-walker. The greatest funambulist of them all lies in Kensal Green Cemetery. His name was Jean François Gravelet, though he performed as 'Blondin', and he is buried with both of his wives (no juggling there – the first, Charlotte, died long before the second, Katharine, arrived). It's a great monument, to be found by the path in square 140 of the cemetery plan: Grade II listed pink Peterhead granite, topped by a tall draped statue of the figure of Hope who sadly, has now lost her anchor. Blondin's white portrait in bas-relief, hair abundant, goatee neat, faces

Jensen

that of Charlotte (no goatee). The only clue to what he did was his place of death: Niagara Falls House in Ealing.

Blondin invented crossing Niagara on a rope. He did it first in 1859, the rope 50 metres or 160 feet above the water, nearly half a kilometre long and 7.5cm, or 3 inches, in diameter. Then he did it again, and again, until he'd notched up seventeen goes. He did it while blindfolded, pushing a wheelbarrow, on stilts, feats that made him famous and were watched by huge crowds. Flamboyant, fearless and theatrical, he would stop mid-way to take photographs of the crowd photographing him. He even walked across Niagara while carrying his assistant, Romain Mouton, who must have been quite mad to agree to it. The Prince of Wales was watching, but when asked by Blondin if he could carry him, did the sensible thing. But the stunt that takes my breath away – not least because it is so French – was when he did it carrying a small stove, stopping mid-way to prepare and cook an omelette, which he then ate. Voilà le petit déjeuner!

Blondin, born in France, worked in America before moving to London. His appetite for funambulising was insatiable, his desire to give his audiences a thrill extending to a stunt at Crystal Palace in which he walked on a tightrope 180 feet above the concrete floor, pushing a wheelbarrow that contained his five-year-old daughter Adele, who dropped rose petals on the audience. Everyone watching was scandalised and the Home Secretary ordered him not to do it again. He didn't, though I suspect he wanted to.

Oh the spectacle of it all! I am not sure what the modern equivalent would be. This is how Charles Dickens, writing for his weekly, *All the Year Round*, in June 1861, described going to see Blondin:

I have just arrived at the Crystal Palace, somewhat ashamed of myself, to see Blondin, the Franco-American rope-dancer, risk his life for my half hour's amusement. I am with some thousands of others, jostling cravers for the unhallowed excitement, and a great choice of delight lies before me. Shall I sit down in the great transept 100 feet below the rope, which looks as small from there as a perch of a bird-cage, and quietly watch till the hero slips and smashes into a red sop of flesh and bones at my feet? Or, shall I go up to the first gallery, where I shall actually be able to see him half way in his fall, and behold his death more pleasantly and tranquilly? Or, shall I risk a little more trouble for an exquisite and new sensation, and ascend to the third, or five shilling gallery? Or, shall I boldly take a gold piece and mount till I can be on a level with the rope of the venturous Icarus and there, watching his lithe and clasping feet, have the felicity of being able for years to lean across the epergne at dinner parties to relate how I was the first to see Blondin's foot miss its hold, the instant before he fell 100 feet, and was picked up stone dead? I know all this is rather cruel, and I am rather ashamed of myself; but really no one can conceal that we all, thousands of us, have come to see an acrobat perform a feat of imminent danger. For an instant, I feel one of a pack of ten thousand staghounds, who are in full cry and thirsting to lap the blood of one poor fox…

Dickens needn't have worried. Blondin outlived him by some years, dying of diabetes at the age of seventy-three, having married his young nurse Katharine two years before. Funambulist indeed.

# FREDERICK HITCH

## SOLDIER
### 29 November 1856–6 January 1913
*Old Chiswick Cemetery, behind St Nicholas' Churchyard,*
*Chiswick Mall, London W4 2PJ*

This grave stopped me in my tracks as I walked down the main path of Old Chiswick Cemetery. It is more monument than anything else: a boulder the size of a horse, a stone helmet resting on top. The inscription says: 'To the memory of Frederick Hitch, VC'. The monument was erected by public subscription to honour his heroic actions at Rorke's Drift in 1879. There is a white stone replica of the VC and a cross with a poppy. Someone has left a paper with the words to the *Ballad of the Victoria Cross*:

> I am the pride of the valiant Brave:
> I am the shame of the coward knave:
> Look tho' the world – Is there prouder need
> Than the plain bronze Cross of the golden deed.

I had to know more. Fred Hitch was twenty-two, a private in the 2<sup>nd</sup> Battalion, 24<sup>th</sup> Regiment of the Foot (later the South Wales Borderers), when he found himself at Rorke's Drift. He received the VC for keeping communications with the hospital open and fighting off the Zulus for seven hours despite being severely wounded, his arm useless by the end. His account of that day begins:

> We did not expect any fighting that day, and were occupied in our usual duties, little thinking that a horde of Zulus – the pick of the Zulu Army, in fact – were marching on us, determined to kill every man at our little post. About one

o'clock two men galloped to the drift, bringing the news that the Zulus had annihilated our force at Isandhlwana, that they were now marching on to attack our post at Rorke's Drift. Lieutenant Bromhead, who was in charge of the post, and Commissioner Dalton at once held a conference. The position was a difficult one: our little force only consisted of a handful of men, whilst the approaching Zulus, mad with success, must have numbered at least four thousand. And many of them, moreover, were armed. At first it was thought the better part of valour to desert the post, but fortunately this decision was altered. We were to defend the post, and hold it at all costs.

And so they did. Fred Hitch returned a hero, if a disabled one, his wounds so severe that he was discharged. He was also illiterate and all of this made it hard to find a steady job. There was bad luck when his Victoria Cross, which he always wore, was stolen. Eventually a replacement was made but that too disappeared, though it turned up later at an auction. His fortunes changed when he began to drive a horse-drawn carriage taxi and later a car. He remains the only taxi driver to have won the VC and is remembered still with the Fred Hitch Gallantry Award. It is his fellow drivers who have made sure that he is not forgotten and it is a magnificent monument. Fred Hitch may have had his share of bad luck but, in death, he is forever a hero, as everyone who walks by knows.

# WILLIAM HOGARTH

## PAINTER AND SATIRIST
### 10 November 1697–26 October 1764
*St Nicholas' Churchyard, Chiswick Mall, London W4 2PJ*

To visit William Hogarth's grave you will, at some point, have to encounter the eponymous roundabout. Here in Chiswick you can walk down Hogarth Lane and visit Hogarth House, but by far the most famous namesake of all is the roundabout, a cacophony of traffic involving the A316 and the A4, encountered by millions as they attempt to enter, or escape, London. (I must admit that I found it quite funny that there is a roundabout named after the great satirist, but I fear that Mr Hogarth would not be amused.)

He was, of course, a genius engraver and satirist, the first and best graphic novelist. His morality tales are acute, detailed and obsessive observations of human foible and misdeed. A personal favourite is his *Four Prints from an Election* of 1754, with its coruscating depiction of political corruption (oh how I wish someone would do one today). Perhaps his greatest morality tale of all was *Marriage à la mode*, which hangs in the National Gallery and depicts the ill-considered marriage (for money) of Earl Squander's son. Here, in six paintings, he charts the perilous path created by greed. It ends, as it must, for Hogarth wasn't in the business of having a heart, with the son being fatally wounded by his wife's lover. She then commits suicide.

I am not sure what I was expecting of the grave, which lies close to the ancient and beautiful St Nicholas parish church in Chiswick, but certainly something a bit maverick. Instead I found the opposite. The sarcophagus is an imposing affair, staid and traditional, self-regarding, a bit too proud and designed with posterity in mind. His great friend, David

Garrick, composed a poem for it to which you can only say 'oh dear':

Farewell great Painter of Mankind
Who reach'd the noblest point of Art
Whose pictur'd Morals charm the Mind
And through the Eye correct the Heart.

If Genius fire thee, Reader, stay,
If Nature touch thee, drop a Tear:
If neither move thee, turn away,
For Hogarth's honour'd dust lies here.

But I did a little more reading and found my own morality tale for this story. For it seems William Hogarth was not content to be a genius satirist. He wanted to prove himself as a painter, of great historical scenes, of royalty, of portraits. He devoted many years to this quest, with some success but also some major failures, and, as a result, was never satisfied. 'He swerved between elation and anxiety, becoming more prone to anger or melancholy in times of stress,' says his biographer Jenny Uglow. 'He worked with his fellow artists and then turned on them, feeling isolated and misunderstood. All the time, he nervously assessed his achievement.' He was often mocked by others, who criticised his vanity, envy and malevolence. So there you have it: William Hogarth: unhappy, bitter, angry. He was able to pinpoint the faults of so many others, but not his own, at least not in a constructive way. I wonder how he would have portrayed that and what other kind of gravestone he could have had. Still, it is a fearsome roundabout.

# FREDERICK RICHARDS LEYLAND

## SHIP-OWNER AND ART COLLECTOR
### 30 September 1831–4 January 1892
*Brompton Cemetery, Fulham Road, London SW10 9UG*

How did Frederick Leyland, Liverpool shipping magnate and arts patron extraordinaire, get into this book? Well, I was walking through Brompton Cemetery after visiting Emmeline Pankhurst, as you do, when I came across the most beautiful tomb that I have ever seen. Grave or jewel-box? This seemed to be both. Surrounded by fine wrought iron railings, spearheaded with lilies, the tall, slender chest is raised up on four Romanesque legs, its pitched copper roof made of rounded tiles, overlapping like fish scales. All sides are decorated with beautiful copper floral scrollwork, as intricate and delicate as embroidery. Raised lettering, running along one side says: 'Here lies Frederick Richards Leyland, sometime of Woolton Hall Liverpool and XLIX Princes Gate.'

Here lies indeed. For this tomb is by Edward Burne-Jones, and it is his only work of funerary art. This may be a grave but it is also a masterpiece and I cannot believe that it isn't in a museum. But there it is, just off the beaten path, in Brompton Cemetery. But then, as I soon discover, Frederick Leyland loved to dazzle, to impress, to own things that made your eyes go wide, your spirit lift (and your admiration for him grow). He was a classic self-made man: the son of a Liverpool bookkeeper, he started working as an apprentice on the Bibby line of steamships when he was fifteen and, when he was twenty-eight, he bought out his employers. Thus the Leyland line, which later started transatlantic services, was born. But Leyland didn't just want to be rich, he wanted to be cultured and set out to transform his homes, in Liverpool and London. He was after what we would now call the 'wow factor', filling his homes with a dazzling array of Italian Renaissance paintings and Pre-Raphaelite works. Leyland's dream, as reported by *Harper's New Monthly Magazine* in 1891, was to live the life of an old Venetian merchant, transposed to the London of the time.

The great painter James McNeill Whistler called Leyland 'The Medici of Liverpool'. Leyland commissioned works from Rossetti, Burne-Jones and Whistler. Indeed, so numerous do the portraits of Leyland and his family seem now that posing must have been almost a full-time occupation. Whistler, an American ex-pat in London, was commissioned often, most famously to decorate the dining room at Leyland's London house at 49 Prince's Gate. This would become known as the Peacock Room, after the birds painted on the shutters and walls. The idea was to showcase Leyland's collection of china but Whistler got carried away, creating a masterpiece in vivid blue-greens and gold leaf, and, in the process, going wildly and persistently over budget.

This was to be their undoing and the falling out was volcanic.

'Ah, I have made you famous,' Whistler is supposed to have said to Leyland 'My work will live when you are forgotten. Still, per chance, in the dim ages to come, you will be remembered as the proprietor of the Peacock Room.' Whistler, who blamed Leyland for his bankruptcy, subsequently drew vitriolic caricatures of him, including one which is memorably titled *The Gold Scab: Eruption in Filthy Lucre*. Whistler was a man who knew how to carry a grudge. Leyland, for his part, kept the Peacock Room, which now can be seen at the Smithsonian in Washington DC.

Leyland died suddenly in 1892, as *The Times* recorded in its death notices: 'On the 4th of January at the Blackfriars station of the District Railway, very suddenly of syncope, Frederick Richard Leyland of 49 Prince's Gate, South Kensington, and Woolton Hall, Liverpool.' I could find no obituary but the newspaper did carry his will, his estate being worth £916,153 10s 10d.

In the end, Whistler was right, in one way. Leyland was famous for having owned the Peacock Room. But I have seen Whistler's grave in Old Chiswick Cemetery, with draped figures integrated into the four corners of the raised tomb. It is not in the churchyard proper, but in the larger cemetery, to the right of the path as you leave the churchyard, next to a brick wall. It is a perfectly good grave but not a patch on the beauty that belongs to Frederick Richards Leyland's tomb, there to be admired by all who pass by.

# KARL HEINRICH MARX

## POLITICAL THEORIST
### 5 May 1818–14 March 1883
*Highgate Cemetery (East), Swains Lane, London N6 6PJ*

It is an incredible fact that, according to his lifelong friend Frederick Engels, there were just nine people at Karl Marx's funeral on 17 March 1883, though admittedly those nine oozed quality. We know this because Engels wrote a report of the funeral in *Der Sozialdemokrat*, the German socialist paper. The funeral was not, I note with no surprise, reported in *The Times* of London but the paper of record did run a short obituary a few days later that began: 'Our Paris correspondent informs us of the death of Dr Karl Marx, which occurred last Wednesday, in London.'

The *Sozialdemokrat* was much more forthcoming. Engels listed those at the funeral, other than himself, as Marx's daughter Eleanor, his two French socialist sons-in-law, three German socialist activists, a British zoologist and a professor of chemistry from Manchester. The small group gathered round his original gravestone, a humble marker that he shared with his wife, who had died fifteen months earlier. (The slab is still there, not that far from his gargantuan monument, and is marked on the cemetery visitors' map.) In general, I suspect that fairy tales and socialism don't mix terribly well but, from the report in *Der Sozialdemokrat* on 22 March 1883, this really did sound like a fairy tale socialist funeral.

Wreaths with red ribbons from *Sozialdemokrat* and the London Communist Workers' Educational Society were laid on the coffin. Engels made a great speech – in English:

On 14 March, at a quarter to three in the afternoon, the greatest living thinker ceased to think. He had been left alone for scarcely two minutes, and when we came back we found him in his armchair, peacefully gone to sleep – but forever. An immeasurable loss has been sustained both by the militant proletariat of Europe and America and by historical science, in the death of this man. Just as Darwin discovered the law of development of organic nature, so Marx discovered the law of development of human history: the simple fact, hitherto concealed by an overgrowth of ideology, that mankind must first of all eat, drink, have shelter and clothing, before it can pursue politics, science, art, religion.

Engels continued: 'Marx was the best-hated and most calumniated man of his time.' And then he declared: 'He died beloved, revered and mourned by millions of revolutionary fellow-workers – from the mines of Siberia to California, in all parts of Europe and America – and I make bold to say that though he may have had many opponents he had hardly one personal enemy. His name will endure through the ages, and so also will his work!'

Oh, imagine the scene as that exclamation marked the spot. An address, from the Russian Socialists, was read out, in French, to the 'Master among all the socialists of our Times'. It included a call that Marx and Engels had sent out to the world thirty-five years before: 'Proletarians of all countries, unite!' Two telegrams from the French and Spanish Workers' Parties were read out. There was a speech from a German comrade: 'He was the best hated but he was also the best loved.'

And then, we must assume, they all went to the pub.

Hated or loved, Marx was not yet famous. It is said that Marx had wanted a simple grave. Engels, when he died, decades later in 1895, had his ashes scattered in the sea near Beachy Head in Eastbourne. I cannot imagine what Marx would think now of his Highgate tomb, which towers, like some sort of breakaway relic of the great gargantuan statues

of the old Soviet Union, over all other mere mortals buried in
the eastern half of the cemetery. The grave was moved after
visitors complained they could not find the original and so,
in 1954, the now defunct Communist Party of Great Britain
commissioned the huge bronze head above the granite plinth
that stands there now. The plinth exhorts 'Workers of all
lands unite' (the first line in *The Communist Manifesto*). And,
on the base, this from the eleventh thesis on Feuerbach: 'the
philosophers have only interpreted the world in various ways
– the point however is to change it.'

Would he even recognise himself as an icon? Or, shudder,
a tourist attraction? Still, he would probably get a kick out
of the fact that he is facing his intellectual nemesis Herbert
Spencer – they are opposites even in death. Around him,
there are a number of revolutionary graves including those
of SWAPO (South West African Peoples Organization) and
the South African Communists. I was delighted to find,
among all of these initials from far-flung lands, the grave of
Paul Foot, the great campaigning journalist who died in 2004.
'Writer and Revolutionary' it says, along with this quote
from Shelley:

> RISE LIKE LIONS AFTER SLUMBER
> IN UNVANQUISHABLE NUMBER
> SHAKE YOUR CHAINS TO EARTH LIKE DEW
> WHICH IN SLEEP HAD FALLEN ON YOU
> YE ARE MANY – THEY ARE FEW.

Over 1,000 people attended Paul's funeral.

Marx shares his grave with his wife Jenny, their daughter,
grandson and Helena Demuth, the housekeeper who was
also their lifelong friend (and his supposed mistress). But shar-
ing a grave with an icon has a price: the human stories here
have been eclipsed. Here the personal is not political; it is

forgotten. The grave has become a magnet for visitors from China in particular. How many zillions of photographs have they taken over the years? Every year, on the anniversary of his death, there is a ceremony at the grave with diplomats from Vietnam, Cuba and China coming to pay their respects. Speeches are given. Wreaths are laid. According to the London Communists website, some 200 people attended this ceremony in 2012.

But would Marx recognise what he has become?

# EMMELINE PANKHURST (NÉE GOULDEN)

## POLITICAL ACTIVIST
### 15 July 1858–14 June 1928
*Brompton Cemetery, Fulham Road, London SW10 9UG*

Her grave is graceful, a Celtic cross in red sandstone, to the left as you walk down the tree-lined avenue from the Old Brompton Road entrance at the cemetery. On it there is carved a long-robed figure, a halo and a duo of flying angels. Most graves look cold; this is warm, with a romantic feel, influenced by art nouveau. Perhaps this is fanciful, but it seems almost Parisian, which would be a good fit for Emmeline Pankhurst because she went to school and sought refuge there, too, when things got too crazy at home. She often insisted that her true birth date was one day earlier, on 14 July, Bastille Day: so born a revolutionary, although in Manchester. It is not a grand grave, feminine in comparison, say, to Marx's monument, and yet it can be argued that here lies Britain's most successful political activist, ever.

The inscription surprises for it says 'Emmeline Pankhurst, wife of R. M. Pankhurst'. That's it. No epitaph. No reference to a life devoted to changing the world, a struggle that, after the turn of the century, turned militant. 'The argument of the broken window pane is the most valuable argument in modern politics,' she said, sending hundreds of women out to do just that. We all have an image of the suffragettes as women in hour-glass Edward gowns and large hats, marching in their thousands, carrying banners, calling for a right that is now universally accepted as just. But we forget about the arson, the break-ins, the relentless violence of the movement, led by Mrs Pankhurst, as she was always known, with an autocracy that belied her love of democracy. She was devoted to the cause, imprisoned many times, each time going on hunger strike, only to be released and re-arrested. This rather lovely Celtic cross gives no clue to a life lived on the barricades.

In a perfect world, perhaps, the world's most famous suffragette probably wouldn't be described on her grave as 'wife of'. But there is no doubt Emmeline Pankhurst would have wanted it that way. She had a paradoxical life: a radical political spirit but also a devoted wife, the mother of five children and a home-maker. 'Not the bitterest critic of Mrs Pankhurst ever suggested that her husband did not find her, from beginning to end of the nineteen years of their marriage, a perfect wife,' says Rebecca West in her essay on her, called 'Reed of Steel'. Emmeline Goulden was born into a political family and met and married Richard Marsden Pankhurst when she was just twenty-one and he was forty-one. He was a barrister and socialist who would campaign to be an MP with her at his side, fighting for causes such as the abolishment of the House of Lords and, yes, women's suffrage. When he died in 1898, she was devastated and vowed to carry on his work. The year after his death she founded the Women's Franchise League and, in 1903, the Women's Social and Political Union.

Rebecca West gives us a real sense of what she was like as a woman:

There has been no other woman like Emmeline Pankhurst. She was beautiful; her pale face, with its delicate square jaw and rounded temples, recalled the pansy by its shape and a kind of velvety bloom on the expression. She dressed her taut little body with a cross between the elegance of a Frenchwoman and the neatness of a nun. She was courageous; small and fragile and no longer young, she put herself in the way of horses' hooves, she stood up on platforms under a rain of missiles, she sat in the darkness of underground gaols and hunger struck, and when they let her out because she had starved herself within touching distance of death, she rested only for a day

or two and then clambered back on to the platforms, she stag-
gered back under the horses' hooves.

She had three daughters, all political creatures but it was
Christabel who fought by her side for so long. But she managed
to fall out with all of them at times, not least over her decision,
in 1914, to suspend the battle for votes so women could devote
themselves to the war effort, working in factories. The decision horrified her daughter Sylvia, who believed, as did many
in the Labour party, that the war was a catastrophe. It is not
without irony that it was this participation in the war effort
that clinched the issue of women's suffrage: women had given
their all to the country and the country gave back to them.

Emmeline's long years of relentless touring and imprison-
ments took their toll. She died at age sixty-nine and her obituary
in *The Times* played on the complexity of her character.

> With all her autocracy and her grievous mistakes, she was a
> humble-minded, large-hearted, unselfish woman, of the stuff of
> which martyrs are made. Quite deliberately, and having counted
> the cost, she undertook a warfare against the forces of law and
> order, the strain of which her slight and fragile body was unable to
> bear. It will be remembered of her that whatever peril and suffer-
> ing she called upon her followers to endure, up to the extreme
> indignity of forcible feeding, she herself was ready to face, and did
> face, with unfailing courage and endurance of body and mind.

There is a statue of Mrs Pankhurst in Victoria Gardens, the
park next to the Houses of Parliament. I walk by it often and
it is not unusual to find flowers there. The last time I went by,
there was a large wreath of green and purple flowers with
a note: 'From the Conservative Women's Organisation: To
honour all the amazing women who have fought for women's
rights. On the 155th anniversary of Emmeline Pankhurst's
birthday.' Surely, she would be proud.

# MARJORIE PROOPS

## AGONY AUNT
### 10 August 1911–10 November 1996
*Golders Green Jewish Cemetery (also known as Hoop Lane Cemetery), London NW11 7NL*

Dear Marje,

I am writing, as millions did to you during your lifetime, after visiting your grave. It's simple, with just your name and date of death. The slab was originally white and, at the foot of it, there is an upstanding open book: on the first page, it says, in flowing italic, '*Dear Marje, I have a problem…*'

So, Marje, I have a problem … in that your grave, not unlike you, tells us quite a lot and very little at the same time. For starters, there's your name. You were born Rebecca Marjorie Israel in Woking in either 1910 or 1911 (your date of birth was one of many elusive facts). Your father changed it to Rayle in deference to prejudice. And you decided to use your middle name after being taunted in the playground as 'Becky the Jew Girl'. You married Sidney Proops – whom you called Proopsie – in 1935, attracted by his socialism, having become engaged three days after meeting him on the strict understanding that you could continue with your career. At the time, you were a freelance artist: hired by the *Mirror* in 1939 to draw hats, you became a columnist in 1954 and instantly became a star.

'She had glamour, pizzazz and pulling power,' said your obituary. Your advice column became hugely popular, attracting millions of letters over thirty years, from the unhappy, troubled and lonely hearted. 'Dear Marje' was an institution, you were a legend, instantly recognisable with your big round glasses and, for most of the time, a cigarette holder. You were a lifelong socialist, a campaigning journalist and, in the end, one of the great and the good.

Your status appears only to have been enhanced when you revealed to a biographer in 1993 that you'd not been happily married at all and, indeed, had conducted a thirty-year affair with a *Mirror* lawyer. Still, you said you never considered leaving Proopsie. You always said that you would like to die while at work at the *Mirror*. 'Then the cleaners can come and sweep me up.' In the end, your last column was published on a Tuesday and you died less than a week later. Such an amazing colourful full life though, now, your grave is looking a little weathered.

Yours,

A fan

# LIONEL WALTER ROTHSCHILD, 2ND BARON ROTHSCHILD

## SCION AND ZOOLOGIST
### 8 February 1868–27 August 1937
*Willesden United Synagogue Cemetery, Beaconsfield Road,*
*London NW10 2JE*

When you hear the name Rothschild, you think that whatever it is attached to has to be grand. The name exudes power and prestige, not to mention wealth on an Alpine scale. A friend had told me about the Rothschild graves and I set off for Willesden with only the vaguest of notions of what I would find. I have to say that the words 'Willesden', hardly the most salubrious area of London, and 'Rothschild' had never been linked in my mind before. The first surprise was the cemetery itself (which, as it is orthodox, requires men to wear hats and women to cover their shoulders). It has a marvellous Victorian feel to it, calm and well-kept, despite being surrounded by relentless London grittiness. The Rothschilds could afford to be buried anywhere but they are here, in a cemetery flanked on one side by a belching, rumbling bus garage and on another by cheek-by-jowl housing and towering flats. It's an area of immigrants, and the Rothschilds know about that though, in their case, it was the nineteenth century and they had a bit of a head start from the family in Frankfurt.

The next surprise was the graves themselves, which are not nearly as grand as I thought they'd be. There are some separate memorials plus three enclosures, the largest of which has eight graves, surrounded by low walls. They are nice but hardly ostentatious, most just with names and dates and Old Testament verses. Among them lies a governor of the bank of England and the first MP and peer who were Jewish. The lord would be Nathan Rothschild, whose father was one of the fabled five sons sent out from Frankfurt by the dynasty's founder Amschel to establish financial empires in Paris, London, Vienna and Naples. The whole tale, of immigrants, wealth, power and prestige, all of which must also be seen in the context that they were Jews, is overwhelming and not a little confusing. I was relieved to find this line from historian Paul Johnson: 'The Rothschilds are elusive. There is no book about them that is both revealing and accurate. Libraries of nonsense have been written about them ... A woman who planned to write a book entitled *Lies about the Rothschilds* abandoned it, saying: "It was relatively easy to spot the lies, but it proved impossible to find out the truth."'

I am saved from adding to the nonsense by the final enclosure which holds the grave of Lionel Walter. 'This is the one who used to ride the carriages pulled by zebras,' explains cemetery worker Alfred, whom I have roped in as a guide. There are well-tended red rose bushes and a stone, with voluptuous stone flowers carved in the base, and a quotation from Job: 'Who teacheth us more than the beasts of the earth, and maketh us wiser than the fowls of heaven?' According to Alfred, of all the Rothschilds it is Walter, as he was called, who gets the most visitors. I suspect that has something to do with the zebra, a beast he undertook to train to prove it could be done, for in Victorian England, an animal that could not be put to work was simply not welcome.

Of course, Walter was supposed to be a banker. Apparently he was required to slog away for years at the family bank (N. M. Rothschild & Sons, you may have heard of it), despite displaying absolutely no ability whatsoever. But that was only the day job. His real love was the natural world. By the age of seven, he had told his parents: 'Momma, Poppa, I am going to make a museum.' By the age of ten, he had enough objects to open one, in the garden shed. But, as he lived in the monumental mansion in capacious Tring Park, it wasn't just any shed. And, by the time he was in his early twenties, he opened a real museum, in Tring, with cases and cases of stuffed birds and butterflies.

He was a trundling bear of a man, 20 stone, with a beard and a stutter. He was shy and never married, though he did have two mistresses, one of whom seemed to excel at being a blackmailer. But according to his great-great niece Hannah, a film-maker who has written about him, his only real loves were his mother Emma and his animals, dead or alive. Walter's success as a collector can be attributed to three things: he had an obsessive interest, wealth and an ability to coordinate a global network of collectors. When I say obsessive, what I mean is utterly possessed. You only have to go to Tring, now a part of the Natural History Museum, with its ceiling to floor glass cases, holding a Noah's Ark-plus horde of animals, birds and insects, to see this. The cassowary, a large colourful bird which seems like something out of *Alice in Wonderland*, held a particular fascination for him. He even had their skins, after being treated, painted in the original colours.

His was the largest natural history specimen collection ever assembled by one person and it included, among other things, 20,000 birds' eggs, two million sets of butterflies and moths, 30,000 bird skins and 144 giant tortoises. Animals named in his honour include a giraffe, porcupine, rock wallaby, hare, fish, lizard and, of course, cassowary. Most of his objects arrived dead but he also kept a menagerie in the grounds at Tring. Hannah relates her great aunt Miriam's description of what the daily walk entailed:

There were fallow deer in the park. There were kangaroos, there were emus and rheas and cassowaries although the cassowaries had disgraced themselves so they were put into a part of the park we no longer really walked in. And the emus were the birds which frightened me the most because they made a curious drumming sound with their feet and followed the prams because they hoped to get food. They had nasty gimlet-like eyes and long beaks and they terrified me.

There were other aspects to his life. He was, for instance, an MP (Conservative) at the end of the century. It was he who received the letter from the British Foreign Secretary Arthur Balfour, in which the British government declared its support for the establishment in Palestine of a home for the Jewish people. This became known as the Balfour Declaration and the 'home' became Israel. For some people, these things would define their lives. But not Walter. His life was devoted not to people, but to the natural world. When he died, in 1937, he gave his vast collection to the Natural History Museum. His grave may be in Willesden but his heart is in Tring, with his stuffed wayward cassowaries.

# MARGUERITE RADCLYFFE HALL ('JOHN')

## WRITER
### 12 August 1880–7 October 1943
*Highgate Cemetery (West) Swains Lane, London N6 6PJ*

It should come as no surprise that Radclyffe Hall is buried with one of her lovers, her first serious one, the much older Mabel Batten, and Mr Batten to boot. Her life was studded by ménages à trois of one kind or another. The vault is in a prime location on the tangled romantic side of Highgate, in the Circle of Lebanon, approached by the Egyptian Avenue. The name over the vault is Mabel Veronica Batten with the date 1917. On the side of the vault, under the name Radclyffe Hall, there is this:

> … AND, IF GOD CHOOSE
>
> I SHALL BUT LOVE THEE BETTER
>
> AFTER DEATH

It is signed UNA, as in Una Troubridge, who was Mabel's first cousin and who was herself married when Radclyffe Hall fell in love with her. At the time, Hall was with Mabel and it was during an argument about Una that Mabel suffered a cerebral haemorrhage and died. Thus 'John' – as Hall preferred to be called, considering herself an 'invert', to use the sexologist term of the day – and Una began a long search to contact Mabel via a medium. Of course, as was perhaps inevitable, 'John' eventually fell in love again with another woman, Eugenia Souline, a Russian nurse, who moved in with them, much to Una's unhappiness.

It's a soap opera, *Downton Abbey* with cross-dressing. There is a marvellously succinct description of Hall, as seen by Vera Brittain, in a *Times* book review that goes like this:

Rich, country-born, of hunting stock; dissolute father; brain-less thrice-married American mother; handsome, charmful, musical, intelligent, ill-educated, early a lover of women, sexually promiscuous when young, inspired to write by a very deep love affair with an older, married woman [Mabel], tamed to some extent by the rather wishy-washy Una Troubridge, Catholic convert – Radclyffe Hall, died aged sixty of cancer.

None of this explains why her grave is visited so much, her memory cherished, her tomb restored by admirers. John was a serious writer, winning prizes and plaudits for novels like *The Unlit Lamp* and *Adam's Breed*. But she is famous now solely as the author of *The Well of Loneliness*, the first lesbian novel, as it is known. It was banned at a notorious trial, which is prob-ably also why we know of it now, though its sex scenes hardly merit the term, ending as they do with the words 'and that night they were not divided'. John did not let the ban defeat her: she continued to write and live life as only she could. I loved this summation in the *Times* obituary on 11 October 1943: 'Radclyffe Hall had abundant sympathy and pity, and views on her controversial book should not be allowed to rob her of credit for her sterling literary qualities, her well-controlled emotional pitch, her admirable prose style. Her interests included psychical research and the breeding of dogs.'

There is a charming 'afterword' to all of this. For the tomb, over the years, fell into disrepair: damp, bricked up, the coffin damaged by Satanists. To fix it two women, Monica Still and Marya Burrell, spent years raising £7,000. It seems that the two women had had an affair when they were aged nine-teen in Hastings (at the time Hall lived in nearby Rye). They parted but were reunited, more than thirty years later in 1972, after Monica appeared in a TV advert for Pedigree Chum and Marya recognised her. They lived together in Kent and, when Marya died in 1988, Monica carried on fundraising. Thus, at the age of seventy-one, on the 51st anniversary of Hall's death, Monica Still was able to preside over a small ceremony at the restored vault, telling *The Independent* that they had done it out of gratitude to Hall for being so brave and ahead of her time. The vault was restored and Hall's coffin was encased in a new oak casket. 'John was a great lover of English oak,' Ms Still mused.

# RICHARD 'STONEY' SMITH

## MILLER
### 16 February 1836–28 August 1900
*Highgate Cemetery (East), Swains Lane, London N6 6PJ*

This is a classic example of someone who had only one great idea but, with genius marketing and luck, made it last forever. Richard Smith was born the son of Richard Smith, a miller, in Stone in Staffordshire, which explains his nickname. But there is also something quite satisfying about a miller named Stoney. His obsession was wheat germ. In the early nineteenth century, brown bread contained more nutrients than white but it soured quickly. Stoney, over a process which we must assume took years, managed to find a way of extracting the wheat germ, steaming it to preserve the nutrients, adding a bit of salt, and then putting it back into the flour, intensifying the nutrients. This resulted in an ultra-wheat germ loaf – a superfood of its time. It would prove to be the best thing since sliced bread.

He teamed up with a firm of millers, S. Fitton and Son, in Macclesfield, and the patent for Smith's Patent Germ Flour was granted in 1887. And there, frankly, is where the story may have ended as it is doubtful we'd all still be buying something called Smith's Patent Germ Bread. But in 1890 Stoney and Thomas Fitton launched a national competition to find a new name. A man called Herbert Grime, who was from Oxford, either a student or a schoolmaster, according to different accounts, won the £25 prize with the name Hovis, a shortened version of the Latin *hominus vis* – the strength of man. The runner-up, by the way, was Yum Yum. I think we know what would have happened if that had been chosen.

In 1896 Thomas Fitton purchased Imperial Mills on the Embankment in London (this is where Millbank takes its name from). The instinct to trade on the healthiness of the bread was there from the start and, in 1889, when cycling was popular, thousands of Hovis Cycle Road Maps and Guides were published to advertise the bread, mapping out teashops where it could be enjoyed. Stoney Smith, a board member, must have moved to London as well, which would explain his grave being in Highgate. His gravestone, a crag of hewn stone that is set back from the path, just before you get to Marx, says:

AFTER YEARS OF PATIENT INVESTIGATION HE PATENTED ON
6 OCTOBER 1887 HIS IMPROVED TREATMENT OF THE WHEAT
GERM AND BROKEN WHEAT WHICH MADE THE MANUFACTURE OF
HOVIS BREAD POSSIBLE.

So there you have it: a man named Stoney who is commemorated on a roughly hewn stone in commemoration of a process involving a millstone. Some things just seem almost perfect.

# SIR JOHN SOANE

## ARCHITECT
### 10 September 1753–20 January 1837
*Old St Pancras Churchyard, Pancras Road, London NW1 1UL*

.It is not everyone who gets to design their own tomb and
then visit it for years before, as it were, the final journey. But
then Sir John Soane, architect and collector extraordinaire,
was not everyone. His house in Lincoln's Inn Fields, crammed
with paintings, architectural gems, domed ceilings and even a
varnished skull, is regarded as one of the best museums in the
world. Indeed, among his objects is the alabaster sarcophagus
of Seti I, the Egyptian pharaoh, who died in 1279 BC, and
which was bought in 1824 from the Italian adventurer Belzoni
for £2,000. Those were the days when England really did
think it ruled the world, in life and death. The sarcophagus,
carved in one piece, covered in amazing figures and hiero-
glyphics inlaid in blue copper sulphate, arrived in 1825 and
Sir John promptly threw a three-day party (wake does not
quite cover it as the mummy, thankfully, was not included).
He invited 890 people, including Prime Minister Robert Peel,
and lit his home with 100 lamps and candelabra. This object
belonged in the Valley of the Kings but ended up in a basement (if an extremely grand one) in London.

I try to imagine, as I look at the Soane tomb in St Pancras
Old Church Graveyard, what it would look like if ripped out
of this green and peaceful English graveyard and placed in
the Valley of the Kings. Nope. I'm not sure it would travel as
well. For this tomb, surely, is the ultimate in English eccen-
tricities. Sir John, a Deist, avoided any Christian symbolism.
Here is the description from Nikolaus Pevsner and Bridget
Cherry's *The Buildings of England*:

Outstandingly interesting monument … extremely Soane-esque, with all his originality and all his foibles. A delicate marble monument beneath a heavy Portland stone canopy. Four piers with incised ionic capitals: a pendentive vault carries a shallow drum encircled by a tail-biting snake (symbol of eternity) with a pineapple shaped finial.

Soane designed the tomb in 1816 for his adored wife Elizabeth (whom he called Eliza), who had died the year before. There is something characteristically wild about the fact that, of all the buildings and monuments that Soane designed (from the Bank of England to the Dulwich Picture Gallery) it is his mausoleum that may have had the most pervasive influence on us. This is because it was the inspiration for the 1926 design for the classic red telephone box by Giles Gilbert Scott, an architect who was also a trustee of the Soane Museum.

Is it this, or is it the pineapple, apparently the symbol in ancient Egypt for regeneration, that makes the Grade I listed tomb seem rather jolly? This, despite the heartfelt inscription to Eliza:

WITH DISTINGUISHED TALENTS SHE UNITED
AN AMIABLE AND AFFECTIONATE HEART.

HER PIETY WAS UNAFFECTED, HER INTEGRITY UNDEVIATING,

HER MANNERS DISPLAYED ALIKE DECISION
AND ENERGY, KINDNESS AND SUAVITY.

THESE, THE PECULIAR CHARACTERISTICS OF HER MIND, REMAINED
UNTAINTED BY AN EXTENSIVE INTERCOURSE WITH THE WORLD.

Their son John was also interred there in 1823. Sir John joined him in 1837, dying estranged from their other, surviving son, George.

The final curiosity of this story, the twist in the stone serpent's tail, or tale, as it were, is that in 2010 it was discovered that a stone capital from the tomb was for sale on eBay – for £4,000! After being reported to the police, the piece was soon returned. I was told this story by a volunteer at St Pancras, who thought it ironic that the man who inspired the telephone box, and thus modern communication, should himself fall foul of such a modern phenomenon. But for me the real irony is that Sir John, a man who delighted in acquiring Seti I's sarcophagus, would himself be the victim of a little tomb robbery.

# DAVID EDWARD SUTCH
# ('SCREAMING LORD SUTCH')

## POLITICIAN AND MUSICIAN
### 10 November 1940–16 June 1999
*Pinner New Cemetery, Pinner Road, Pinner HA5 5RH*

There is something quite perfect about David Sutch or, as he styled himself, Screaming Lord Sutch, 3rd Baronet of Harrow, being buried in Pinner, the epitome of suburban outer-London obscurity. He was the classic English eccentric, the man who gave us the Loony Party, the oddball with the megaphone and the top hat, festooned with buttons, on the fringe of what seemed like every significant by-election in the 1980s. There really cannot be many people buried in Pinner whose death was reported in the following way: 'Downing Street has led the tributes to Lord Sutch, the leader of the Official Monster Raving Loony Party, who has been found dead at his London home. He was fifty-eight.' I think that he would have been impressed.

When I visited his grave, which he shares with his mother Nancy, to whom he was devoted, it was festooned with an ancient, decaying top hat, tinged an alien green from lichen, and the remains of a CD by Doppelherz, a tribute to Lord Sutch's first career (I am not counting his time as a window cleaner) in the early 1960s as a pioneer of horror rock. This is how Lord Sutch would later describe how he was discovered. 'I was doing the horror,' he said, 'screaming and yelling. I had eighteen inches of hair and I was running around in buffalo horns and my auntie's leopard-skin coat. The scout said "You've got a different approach. You want to make a record?"' He did. Early subject matter revolved around coffins and graveyards. (I blame Dickens, whom his mother loved, for naming him after David Copperfield, for the great writer loved a good graveyard).

Indeed the 'song' that was left on his grave, which Doppelherz had covered, was called 'Jack the Ripper', which Sutch performed with huge theatricality, murdering one or another of his band-mates before throwing hearts and livers (from the butchers, thank God) into the audience.

Politics would prove a little less bloody. He first stood as a candidate, for the National Teenage Party, in 1963 in Stratford-upon-Avon, the by-election called after the Profumo scandal. It wasn't until the 1980s, when he founded the Loonies, that he found fame. This was the Thatcher era. Indeed, he ran against her in East Finchley in 1983. Bizarrely, though that word seems slightly superfluous in his case, at one point, he considered changing his name to Margaret Thatcher, but decided that it would be too confusing (I am not sure for whom). His slogans were memorable – 'Vote for insanity, you know it makes sense' – but many of the early policies (the right to vote at eighteen, the launch of commercial radio, passports for pets, knighthoods for The Beatles) did eventually catch on. He stood for election thirty-nine times, a perpetual figure of fun, the pricker of pomposity, the clown at the edge of the count.

The Loonies continue without him, often turning out to be surprisingly sane and always enlivening the political scene. His death was sad (he suffered from depression and the death of his mum in 1997 hit him especially hard) but his epitaph on his grave, which is in section J2, on the outside edge, says it all:

A LORD WITHOUT PEER
SUTCH IS THE WAY
IT WAS WITH HIM
AND SUTCH IS WHY
HE'LL ALWAYS BE WITH US

And always be in Pinner too.

# GEORGE JAMES SYMONS

## METEOROLOGIST
### 6 August 1838–10 March 1900
*Kensal Green Cemetery, Harrow Road, London W10 4RA*

It had been a warm, drizzly day that just got wetter and wetter until, as we walked around Kensal Green, it seemed as if the raindrops were as large as balloons. The paths were flooded. My shoes were hopelessly swamped. We were wet, wet, wet. But I must say that I think George James Symons, whose grave was also getting soaked, would have approved. For Mr Symons is the man who invented the way we measure the rain in Britain. He is Mr Rainfall, the original Rain Man. It was in 1858 that Mr Symons elevated British rain from the sphere of small talk and made it a proper study of mankind. You know how the meteorologists now always say: 'It's the wettest day since records began'? Well Mr Symons was the one who got them going.

It all started in the garden of his house in Camden, a house that revolved around the barometer and not the clock. *The Times* records, in an article commemorating the Symons rain measuring centenary of 1958, that 'whenever there was any great depression in the meteorological sense, he would sit up till nearly midnight taking readings every fifteen minutes'. He somehow managed to get hundreds and hundreds of others in Britain to join him, for no money, in his pursuit of measuring rain. He published the first edition of what would become his annual *Britain Rainfall* in 1860: it contained statistics from 168 other unpaid observers. By 1898, this had increased to 3,404. He commanded this unpaid army of observers for free from his home where, incidentally, he kept a library of 14,000 works on the weather. He also had a great interest in the existence, or not, of thunderbolts.

His tombstone, in square 130, row three of Kensal Green, was renovated by the Royal Meteorological Society in 2010, after the original became too weathered (which he would probably have understood). It is made of slate donated by Honiston Slate Mine in Cumbria, which may be the wettest place in Britain, though actually, on the particular afternoon I visited, I suspect that the wettest place was Kensal Green Cemetery. The stone identifies George James Symons as the 'Founder of the Britain Rainfall Organisation, Pioneer in the scientific study of rainfall, Twice President of the Royal Meteorological Society.' But there is one thing missing from this grave: a Symons Rain Gauge to measure you know what. Surely, this man is a national hero.

*

# LADY JANE FRANCESCA 'SPERANZA' WILDE

## WRITER AND MOTHER
### 27 December 1821–3 February 1896
*Kensal Green Cemetery, Harrow Road, London W10 4RA*

Every woman becomes their mother. That's their tragedy. And
no man becomes his. That's his tragedy.
Oscar Wilde, *The Importance of Being Earnest*

There are many contradictions in the life of Lady Wilde,
the feminist, poet and fervent Irish nationalist. She loved
Ireland but moved to England; she was born plain Jane Elgee
but, after her husband was knighted, was happy to be a lady.
She hated the British government but received a small pension
from them anyway. But perhaps the biggest is that such an
early women's rights campaigner would become famous not
for anything that she had done but because she was mother to
Oscar. He, of course, is buried in Père Lachaise in Paris, with
the magnificent tomb (with missing penis) sculpted by Jacob
Epstein. Hers was a much less celebrated end. She died penni-
less while Oscar was in gaol, having been refused permission
to visit him. Thus, though larger than life while alive (for she
was very tall), she was buried in a common pauper's grave in
Kensal Green. She only got her own marker – in her case, a
Celtic cross – in 2000. This was thanks, again, to her son, as
it was erected by the Oscar Wilde Society.

I like the location: very wild if not Wildean, bordering one edge
of the cemetery, in square 147, surrounded by a riot of greenery.
She appears as Lady Wilde, née Elgee, and as 'Speranza' of
*The Nation*, one of her pseudonyms while writing for the Irish
national weekly magazine (another was John Fanshawe Ellis).
She is identified as a writer, translator, poet, nationalist and
early advocate of equality for women and as a wife and mother

to William, Oscar and Isola. After her husband died in 1876, near to bankruptcy, Lady Wilde came to London to live with her eldest son (who was also broke). There she was famous for her soirées or 'At Homes', as they were called, attended by the likes of W. B. Yeats and George Bernard Shaw. She was seen as warm-hearted, romantic and eccentric. Here, writer Catherine Jane Hamilton describes Lady Wilde at home in 1889:

> A tall woman, slightly bent with rheumatism, fantastically dressed in a trained black and white checked silk gown. From her head floated long white streamers; mixed with ends of scarlet ribbon. What glorious dark eyes she had. Even then, and she was over sixty, she was a strikingly handsome woman. Her talent for talk was infectious; everyone talked their best ... 'I cannot write,' I heard her say, 'about such things as Mrs Green looked well in black and Mrs Black looked very well in green!'

Oscar wrote in *De Profundis*:

> My mother, who knew life as a whole, used often to quote to me Goethe's lines – written by Carlyle in a book he had given her years ago, and translated by him, I fancy, also:–
>
> Who never ate his bread in sorrow,
> Who never spent the midnight hours
> Weeping and waiting for the morrow –
> He knows you not, ye heavenly powers
>
> They were the last lines which that noble Queen of Prussia, whom Napoleon treated with such coarse brutality, used to quote in her humiliation and exile; they were the lines my mother often quoted early in the troubles of her later life.

So now, finally, recognition is hers.

# JOHN CONSTABLE

## PAINTER
### 11 June 1776–31 March 1837
*St John-at-Hampstead Churchyard, Church Row, London NW3 6UU*

*See entry for Willy Lott in East of England*

# GEORGE WOMBWELL

## MENAGERIST AND LION-TAMER
### 24 December 1777–16 November 1850
*Highgate Cemetery (West), Swains Lane, London N6 6PJ*

*See Hannah Twynnoy in West of England*

*William Blake, Bunhill Fields*

# LONDON:
## NORTH AND EAST
## OF THE THAMES

● *Cora Crippen*

⊖ EAST FINCHLEY

STOKE NEWINGTON ⇌

●

*Frank C. Bostock,*
*William Calcraft,*
*Joanna Vassa (Bromley)*

● *Joseph Grimaldi*

● *William Blake,*
*John Bunyan*

■ CITY OF LONDON

## WILLIAM BLAKE

### ARTIST AND VISIONARY
### 28 November 1757–12 August 1827

*Bunhill Fields, 38 City Rd, London EC1Y 1AU*

## JOHN BUNYAN

### RELIGIOUS WRITER
### 28 November 1628–31 August 1688

*Bunhill Fields, as above*

I went to visit William Blake and ran into John Bunyan as well. As you do, at least in Bunhill Fields, the Nonconformist graveyard that is a short walk from Old Street tube and has become, quite perfectly, I think, a lunch spot for the achingly hip. It's a place of organised chaos, with almost all of the gravestones, tombs and sarcophagi now tidied up behind iron railings and admonitions not to disturb. So it's not as if you are in a cemetery, it's rather as if you are in front of an elaborate backdrop, almost like a tableau, for al fresco dining.

I see Blake first. Actually he's hard to miss, right in the middle of one of the pathways, a squat, slightly misshapen stone. It is overshadowed by a white obelisk, right next to it, to the prolific Daniel Defoe, author of *Robinson Crusoe* and about 500 other things. It's funny but I'm not interested in Defoe's grave at all. Don't know why but graves are like that. Not only is Blake's stone way less flashy than Dan's pointy monument, it's not even accurate. The stone says: 'Nearby lie the remains of the poet-painter William Blake, 1757–1827 and his wife Catherine Sophia 1762–1831'. Nearby? It doesn't seem good enough, really, not for a gravestone. I do some research. It seems that in 1965 the gravestones were taken away to create a new lawn and someone forgot to mark the exact spot. But, to be honest, I think the great visionary would actually love that.

It's a cool scene. Young men in slim-cut grey suits, earphones in, text as they walk by in their long, thin, pointy leather shoes. Others walk with their bikes, dogs or children in tow. The benches are filled with lunchers. Even the wonderful squattish fig tree with many twisting trunks that shades Blake has a temporary lodger, who leans back, chewing away on a submarine sandwich, surveying the gravestone. Someone has given Blake a plant pot, wrapped in paper. Coins have been left on top, both American and British pennies, plus a small stone, a sort of 'I was here' blessing. On top is a flower, wilting as I watch, not bought but picked from a garden. Blake died almost 190 years ago, his greatness more or less unrecognised, his *Jerusalem* still a poem and not a hymn, much less an Olympic anthem, and yet people still want to keep in touch, to touch him. I guess we all think of him as an eternally modern type of guy.

The bench nearest Blake is occupied by a woman occupied with eating a banquet for one, so I turn around and find a quiet spot at the other end of the path. It's next to a tomb, solid, big, a proper monument, unlike Blake's little stone. 'John Bunyan, author of *The Pilgrim's Progress*,' reads the inscription on the side. He died in August 1688, a good generation ahead of Blake. The tomb is impressive: one side shows a pilgrim, with a heavy burden and a stick, the other has a man raising a cross to the sky. On top there is a recumbent form, as stern in stone as I imagine that Bunyan was in real life. After all this is a man who spent a great deal of time in prison, refusing to repent for his renegade preaching. I'm intrigued by *The Pilgrim's Progress*, which many say is the most popular book ever and written partly from prison. I don't know why but there is something profoundly old-fashioned about the journey of its main character Christian (of course) who goes on a journey from his home on Earth (The City of Destruction) to heaven (The Celestial City). Along the way, the pilgrimage takes in Vanity Fair and the Slough of Despond, meeting the likes of Pliable, Obstinate, Talkative and Mr Worldly-Wiseman. (As someone who covers politics, these are not strangers to me!) I decide that I really should try and read it again.

I look around me. On the bench opposite the tomb, a young woman, blonde, dipping into a bag of crisps, is engrossed in *Fifty Shades of Grey*. I must admit that I almost blush. What would Bunyan think of that? For him, the Room of Pain would never be *that*. Another woman unwraps her sandwich, eyes glued to her Kindle. I imagine that she may be reading *Fifty Shades* as well. I can pretty much guarantee it's not *The Pilgrim's Progress*.

I have bought my lunch, a 'superfood' salad, on the way from a place called Abokado ('Live your life, love our food'). It is so cool that I don't even have cutlery, only chop-sticks. I try to imagine what Bunyan, or Blake, would make of this scene. They wrestled with ideas, divinity and agonised to answer unanswerable questions. We live in shallower times, or so I imagine, though these are the kind of thoughts that cannot help but spring, unbidden, when you have lunch with Blake and Bunyan under the shade of the beautiful, arching, tall green trees of Bunhill Fields.

# WILLIAM CALCRAFT

## EXECUTIONER
### 1800 (date unknown)–13 December 1879
*Abney Park Cemetery, Stoke Newington High Street,*
*London N16 0LH*

I had gone to Abney Park Cemetery to see the grave of William Booth, the founder and 'first general' of the Salvation Army. But as I stood looking at his grave (he has a date of birth and then a date for 'born again'), I happened to overhear a group of young men walking behind me.

One of them said, 'One of my friends found out that one of his relatives is here, a hangman, a really horrible one, who made his victims really suffer.'

Another answered, 'Wow, can you imagine that?'

They tramped by, out of earshot now, but I was intrigued. Here I was, standing in front of the graves of people we can only call the good guys, the founders of an evangelical movement that has helped countless of the poor and needy. And yet, I found myself more interested in the hangman. Who was he? How bad was he? I left my heavenly band of Salvationists and headed off to find out more.

His name was William Calcraft but he was listed in cemetery records as Calcroft, a deliberate misspelling, which, I am told, was not unusual for hangmen as it avoided revenge attacks. John from the Abney Park Visitor Centre guides me to the stone which is down a path from a large statue of hymn writer Isaac Watts, who is, again, I note, definitely one of the good guys. We press on, clambering over stones, resolutely pursuing the darker side of the human race. The grave is not easy to find (number 046783 off Boundary Road) and I would not have spotted it without John. His name is arched at the top of the stone with the main name on it being that of his wife, Louisa.

He was, I discover, a legend, credited with being the most prolific executioner of all time. Born in Essex, he moved to London when he was ten and, after a brush with petty crime, trained as a cobbler. An account of his life from the biography *Groans from the Gallows* that appeared in 1880 in *The Telegraph* says that accident threw him into contact with the public executioner. Calcraft soon became his assistant, gaining the full title in 1828. He would continue until 1874, carrying out between 430 and 450 executions, including the last public execution and the first private one (held in prisons) in 1868. From all accounts – and *The Times* in particular seemed obsessed with reporting executions, which could attract tens of thousands – he was much in demand, a sort of macabre celebrity of his age. As *The Times* wrote of a trip to Dundee, 'If their visitor had been a Royal personage or an eminent statesman he would hardly have been treated with greater consideration.' Such was the excitement that his departure on the train attracted a 'vast crowd'. It adds, 'Calcraft himself, who seemed unmoved by this display of affectionate curiosity, kindly leaned out of the window of a second class carriage in order that all present might have an opportunity of inspecting him and, thus waving his adieu to Dundee, the hangman passed out of sight.'

There seem to be two quite different views of Calcraft. One was that he was a sadist who delighted in prolonging the deaths of his victims. He used the 'short drop' method of hanging which causes the victims to be strangled. There are reports that his victims could take some time to die and that Calcraft sometimes hung on their legs or climbed onto their shoulders to help them along. *The Times* relates a hanging, in Shrewsbury, on 9 April 1869, of John Mapp, a child murderer: 'He said "Goodbye" when Calcraft shook hands with him and, as he left him, he turned his head as if about to speak, but at that moment the drop fell, there was a loud cry from the crowd and all was over. In turning his head round Mapp displaced the rope and the noose was thus brought round almost under his chin, the consequence being that the fall not being immediately fatal, he struggled desperately for half a minute before he died.' But, another hangman history points out that it is unfair to criticise him for the 'short drop' as, during most of his reign, the 'long drop' gallows, with the trap door that allowed the body to fall heavily, thus breaking the neck, was not in common use.

The *Telegraph* article is much kinder about Mr Calcraft, noting that he was naturally of an amiable disposition. He lived in Hoxton and was apparently particularly partial to rabbits (as pets, I hasten to add).

> He loved to pass his leisure and take a friendly glass with other fanciers of those large-eared, sad-eyed pets. One day, however, a brother naturalist made some passing observation or reference to Mr Calcraft's professional avocation, always a subject to be ignored in his presence, where upon he rose from his seat, displeased but not enraged, and gathering up his rabbits, looked reproachfully round and quitted the apartment at once and forever.

He sold the rope from his hangings for 5s to £1 (thus the saying 'money for old rope') and was allowed to sell the clothes of his victims (or 'clients' as *The Telegraph* calls them). 'These articles of apparel Mr Calcraft used to sell to the proprietors of waxwork exhibitions, and he would sometimes grimly chuckle over the fact of an entire change of fashion taking place in consequence of Mrs Manning having expired dressed in black satin.'

It seems that, as he got older, and once he was more or less forced to retire after becoming a serial bungler of executions, he became surly. Indeed, when his mother became a pauper, he had to be ordered to help pay for her support, something he objected to, saying he had three children of his own to support. Thus the *Telegraph* piece notes, 'From which it would seem that though a skilful executioner and kind hearted to rabbits, he was not remarkable for filial affection.'

So not one of the good guys, really. As I leave the cemetery, I walk again past the Salvationists (who do not die but are 'promoted to glory') and feel guilty but not, it must be said, enough to stop.

# CORA CRIPPEN

## MURDER VICTIM
### 1873 (date unknown)–1 February 1910
*Islington and St Pancras Cemeteries, 278 High Road,*
*East Finchley, London N2 9AG*

It is not easy to find Cora Crippen's grave but then surely, I thought, tramping around Section RC7 in this huge cemetery that hugs London's North Circular Road, nothing to do with her would be easy. I drove over to the cemetery office and said I needed help in finding grave 40 in RC7.

'You're looking for Cora Crippen, aren't you?' asked the clerk there.

I admitted I was. She said I wasn't the only one and that Cora's grave, tall and rounded, was easy to find. And then she added, 'You know it's not her, don't you? It's a man.'

Armed now with a plot map and excellent directions, I headed back to RC7 and this time I did find it, though not without a mini battle with the abundant nettles and ivy. The gravestone is rounded, the writing easy to read: 'Cora Crippen (Belle Elmore) who passed away 1 February 1910 RIP'. A fading bouquet and a pink pot plant were by the base.

It is quiet here, green and, yes, peaceful. But RIP? Cora Crippen? I don't think so. For whoever lies here was murdered. There is not a body but just a bit of a body, what was left of the headless corpse found in the coal cellar of the Holloway home where Cora, a wannabe stage artiste, lived with her husband, Dr Hawley Crippen, homeopath and patent medicine salesman. It sounded a nightmare marriage. He was having an affair with his secretary. Cora herself had no shortage of extramarital activities. History records him to be, in his manner, more mouse than man, mild-mannered, polite and small, with spectacles and a moustache. She is portrayed as a loud, flirtatious drinker, a not overly talented music hall singer and dancer. They were both American, having met in New York, where Dr Crippen had come to work as a homeopath. Her original, utterly extraordinary name was Kunigunde Mackamotzki, her mother German, her father Polish. They moved to England in 1897 where she, under the name of Belle Elmore, tried her luck in show business again.

On 1 February 1910 Cora Crippen vanished. His mistress, Ethel Le Neve (another great name), promptly moved in and started wearing her clothes and jewellery. Dr Crippen claimed Cora had gone to America with a lover, then announced that she had died there. George Orwell said this was a story that no fiction writer would ever have made up and here is another detail that astounds: police were first alerted to Cora's disappearance by a friend who was a strongwoman named Vulcana. They searched the house and interviewed Dr Crippen, who, alarmed, fled with Ethel to Brussels, before boarding the SS *Montrose* for Canada.

Police began to search in earnest, eventually finding the headless torso, though it was really more just remains, the head, limbs and spine being absent. It was wrapped in Dr Crippen's pyjama top, plus there was some of Cora's bleached blonde hair in curlers and traces of a poison that Dr Crippen had bought from a chemist before the murder. Meanwhile, on the SS *Montrose*, Crippen was posing as a Mr Robison travelling with his teenage son (Ethel dressed as a boy). The captain saw through her disguise and sent a telegram back to Britain: 'Have strong suspicions that Crippen London cellar murderer and accomplice are among saloon passengers. Moustache taken off, growing beard. Accomplice dressed as boy. Manner and build undoubtedly a girl.' Scotland Yard's Chief Inspector Walter Dew boarded a faster ship, arrived in Canada, and boarded the *Montrose*. Crippen supposedly said 'Thank God it's over' and held out his arms for handcuffs.

At his trial at the Old Bailey, the jury found him guilty after only twenty-seven minutes of deliberation. He was executed at Pentonville Prison on 23 November 1910. He was buried with a picture of Ethel, who, having been acquitted, had fled to America on the day of his death. His grave was unmarked. The scene of the murder has also disappeared, bombed in the First World War.

This leaves us only with this grave and the torso below. In the past decade, there have been new scientific attempts to examine the evidence, with some tests showing that the remains had belonged to a man. DNA tests claimed that the body was no relation to Cora's relatives. But there are many who insist that this evidence is flawed. In 2009, the Criminal Cases Review Commission decided not to hear the case to pardon Crippen. And all that is tangible is an overgrown grave near the North Circular and a mystery that, I believe, will never be solved.

# JOSEPH GRIMALDI

## CLOWN
### 18 December 1778–31 May 1837
*Grimaldi Park, Pentonville Road, London N1 9PE*

Joseph Grimaldi was the great clown of the nineteenth century, indeed the man who invented clowns as we know them: white of face, red of mouth, slapstick of manner, wearing kaleidoscope clothes. His life, at least seen from the relatively safety of modern London, seems fantastical. Here is a taste of it. He was born near the West End as it is now, his parents dancers and performers, and went on the stage at the age of four. His father was a violent brute who was obsessed with his own death. His nickname was Grim-All-Day and he lived in such dread of being buried alive that he insisted in his will that, after his death, he must be beheaded. This wish was fulfilled.

I guess if you had Grim-All-Day as a father then, truly, you might have to laugh to survive. But Joseph Grimaldi, who started on the stage at the age of four, wasn't just funny; he was a comic genius on stage, an intensely creative and anarchic performer who kept thousands in stitches. He re-invented pantomime and specialised in a kind of theatre that does not exist today. Actor Simon Callow, in his review of the marvellous biography *The Pantomime Life of Joseph Grimaldi* by Andrew McConnell Stott, describes Joey's trademark set pieces: 'a non-stop variety show of surreal brilliance in which live ducks flew out of pies, chair and tables hovered 8ft in the air, huge balconies suddenly disappeared, hats turned into bells that started to chime, bottles became buzzing beehives.' The man at the centre of all of this, racing, falling, ducking and diving, was Joey himself. It was incredibly demanding physically and his body gave out at the age of forty-three. From then on he lived, by virtue of an income begot by public subscription, a bizarre existence in which, when he went out, which he did nightly, to reminisce at his local pub before much smaller audiences, he was carried home on the landlord's back. He outlived his son, who died of alcoholism at age thirty, and his wives.

Grimaldi was not only the original clown but the original sad clown. This, then, is the 'joke' often told:

Young man: Doctor, I have been overcome by a terrible sadness.
Doctor: Why not do something happy like go see Grimaldi the clown?
Young man: Ah but Doctor, I *am* Grimaldi.

The coroner ruled that he had died from natural causes or, as it was recorded: 'Died by Visitation of God'. He was buried in the graveyard of St James's Church on Pentonville Road, near what is now King's Cross station. The church is no more but the grave is the star attraction of what is now called Grimaldi Park. It is a quiet place, with benches and gravel. As parks go it is urban gritty, sometimes a bit scruffy, with old gravestones stacked at the sides. His grave is

Grade II listed, surrounded by railings and decorated with the masks of comedy and tragedy. The plaque explains who he was and adds, 'He was adored by all and could fill a theatre anywhere. The name "Joey" has passed into our language to mean a clown. He lived all his life among the people of Clerkenwell.'

When he died, the *London Illustrated News* was moved to write, 'Grimaldi is dead and hath left no peer. We fear with him the spirit of pantomime has disappeared.' But actually, Joey Grimaldi is among the best remembered of all my graves (not least because Charles Dickens edited his memoir, which appeared posthumously). Every February, there is a church service held in his honour: it used to be at St James's but has now moved to Holy Trinity Church in Dalston, where the congregation are actually a bunch of clowns. And before you leave his park, walk towards the road from the grave and look down: you will see two coffin-shaped forms on the ground. This memorial, devised by artist Henry Krokatisis in 2010, labels one coffin as Grimaldi and the other as his friend, dramatist and theatre manager Charles Dibden. The caskets are made up of tiles, which, when walked on, are supposed to play a tune called 'Hot Codlins', one of Joey's hit numbers. When I was there, I did try and dance on this 'grave' but ended up more or less stomping and I could only get a few beeps out of it. Still, I imagine I looked quite funny doing it.

# JOANNA VASSA (BROMLEY)

## DAUGHTER OF OLAUDAH EQUIANO
### April 1795–10 March 1857
*Abney Park Cemetery, Stoke Newington High Street,*
*London N16 0LH*

Joanna Vassa's grave was rediscovered, among the Humpty-Dumpty landscape of tumbledown memorial-abilia in Abney Park Cemetery, in 2005. As Victorian monuments go, it is unremarkable, a draped urn atop a tall column. Her name is indistinct but you can discern 'Vassa', the adopted surname of her father, Olaudah Equiano, the former slave whose book about his life became a bestseller in the 1790s. The grave was restored by 2007, in time for the 200th anniversary of the abolition of the slave trade. She is our only tangible link with Equiano, who died in London in 1797, when Joanna was just two. Her mother Susannah, who was English and white, had died the year before.

We know little about Joanna, whose life as a middle-class, mixed-race woman during this time prompts so many questions. Her father had been born in 1745 to the Igbo tribe in a region now in Nigeria. He was kidnapped at eleven, taken on a slave ship to Barbados, then to Virginia where he was sold to a captain in the Navy and given the name of Gustavus Vassa, the name of a Swedish king, of all things. (The only book on Joanna Vassa, called *Equiano's Daughter*, by Angelina Osborne, notes that enslaved Africans were often given names of powerful historic figures as cruel jokes.)

Equiano was sold again, and again, and eventually bought his freedom in 1766. By now he was educated and busy with many projects as trader, seaman, merchant and explorer (even going on an expedition to the Arctic to find the Northwest Passage). In 1777, in England, he became involved in the plight of the black poor (apparently, and again I owe this to Angelina

Osborne, there were 14,000 blacks in England at the time, many of them former slaves who had thought they would receive land but ended up destitute on the streets of London). He became an active abolitionist, working with Granville Sharpe in the Society for the Abolition of the Slave Trade, speaking at public meetings, describing the cruel realities of life as a slave.

His autobiography, *The Interesting Narrative of the Life of Olaudah Equiano, the African*, caused a sensation when it was published in 1789. Well written, unsparing, evocative, it told of a world of horrors that most had not had the power to imagine. Here, for instance, is his description of his journey to Barbados in the hold of a slave ship:

> The closeness of the place, and the heat of the climate, added to the number in the ship, which was so crowded that each had scarcely room to turn himself, almost suffocated us. The air soon became unfit for respiration, from a variety of loathsome smells, and brought on a sickness among the slaves, of which many died. The wretched situation was again aggravated by the chains, now unsupportable, and the filth of the necessary tubs, into which the children often fell, and were almost suffocated. The shrieks of the women, and the groans of the dying, rendered the whole scene of horror almost inconceivable.

The book became a bestseller and it was also published in Germany in 1790 and, the next year, in America and Holland. Equiano travelled ceaselessly to promote it. His readings were attended by thousands. The book came out the day before William Wilberforce made his first speech in Parliament against the slave trade and it seems to have been *the* book of the time: 'When John Wesley lay dying, it was Equiano's book he took up to reread,' notes writer David Dabydeen.

It was in 1789, when selling and promoting his book, that Equiano met Susannah Cullen. She was a subscriber to the third edition of the book. He wrote to a friend of his intention to marry her, setting out his plans: 'When I have given her about eight or 10 days of comfort, I mean directly to go to Scotland and sell my 5ᵗʰ edition.' Thus Susannah was plunged into a world of travel, promotion, politics and campaigning. They settled near her parents in Soham in Cambridgeshire and had two daughters, Anna, born in 1793 and Joanna, born two years later. It is thought Susannah's parents would have cared for the girls as their father and mother travelled ceaselessly round the country. In 1796, Susannah died and, a year later, in London, Equiano died, aged fifty-two. Later on that year, Anna also died. Thus, at the age of two, Joanna Vassa, as she was known, had lost both parents and her sister.

Equiano, because of his book, died if not rich then certainly well-off. Joanna, as his heir, would have been brought up well, educated, learning to play a musical instrument. It is thought she lived in Soham or nearby. When she turned twenty-one, she inherited £950, a considerable sum then. At twenty-six, she married a man named Henry Bromley. He was a Congregationalist minister and, as Equiano had been religious (he had converted to Methodism), it is assumed that Joanna would have attended church regularly too. It is thought they may have met at church. As a pastor, Henry would probably have been poor. Joanna was not. We do not know if he married for money but that is certainly a possibility.

She and Henry first lived in Appledore in Devon until 1826, moving to Clavering in Essex, where they spent twenty years. It is not clear how Joanna, as a mixed-race woman, was treated. As a minister's wife, she should have had a definite role assisting her husband. That there were tensions of some kind is obvious from the letter of resignation written by Henry in 1845: 'Mrs Bromley's health is very seriously suffering from the injurious influence of the situation, as connected with the peculiar state of her constitution.' They moved to London but, at least by the 1851 census, he was living and working as a pastor in Harwich and Joanna was living in Stowmarket in Suffolk. Sometime in the next few years, she moved to London, without Henry. She died there on 10 March 1857, from 'uterine disease'. Henry was not with her when she died. She was buried in Abney Park, her grave in modern times lost and forgotten, now restored but still prompting more questions than it answers.

## FRANK C. BOSTOCK

### LION-TAMER AND SHOWMAN
### 10 September 1866–8 October 1912
*Abney Park Cemetery, Stoke Newington High Street,*
*London N16 0LH*

See Hannah Twynnoy
in West of England

*Thomas Crapper, Beckenham Cemetery*

# SOUTH
# LONDON

CITY OF LONDON
*Mahomet Weyonomon*
*Cross Bones Graveyard*
SOUTHWARK

*Thomas Crapper,*
*W. G. Grace,*
*Frederick Wolseley*   BECKENHAM

# THOMAS CRAPPER

## INVENTOR
### September 1836–27 January 1910
*Beckenham Cemetery, Elmers End Road,*
*Beckenham, Kent BR3 4TD*

On my way to see Thomas Crapper's grave, in a corner of south-east London, I drove by a sign directing me to the village of Pratt's Bottom and could not help but smile. I remembered that when driving to see Shakespeare's grave in Stratford-upon-Avon, I had seen a sign to North Piddle, which I subsequently discovered was located at Piddle Brook. Of course, it could be even better (or worse, depending on your point of view). There is a little place in Dorset called Shitterton. And then, in Devon, there is Crapstone...

Which brings me back to Mr Crapper. He was born in Yorkshire in 1836, actual date unknown, though he was baptised in September, and came to London to find work when he was twelve, an age which, apparently, wasn't that uncommon. He became a plumbing apprentice and by the age of twenty-five had started his own company, Thomas Crapper and Co., makers of sanitary ware. Now there are all sorts of claims that the word 'crap' as we know it – and use it – is actually of Middle English, Dutch (krappen) or Old French (crappe) origin. But I think that is a revisionista thing and is not giving Mr Crapper his proper place in lavatorial humour, much less history. For, Old French or not, I think that without Mr Crapper and his Valveless Waste Preventer we would not say, as we miss the turn-off to Pratt's Bottom, 'Crap, how did I miss that...?'

There are also people who, when the name Thomas Crapper comes up, immediately tell you that he didn't actually invent the flush toilet. This can be claimed by Sir John

Harrington in 1596 and there are also conflicting stories of patents in the 1770s. But T. Crapper did greatly improve on what existed and held nine patents, one of which was for the floating ballcock (which itself must score high as a source of lavatorial giggles). What cannot be argued with is that at a time when bathroom fixtures were hardly spoken of, T. Crapper, with his flare of sales and promotion, backed by high-quality wares, brought the whole subject out of the (water) closet. His showroom, the first of its kind, was on the King's Road in Chelsea and soon he would add the 'by royal appointment' to his advertisements.

In the 1880s Queen Victoria bought Sandringham house in Norfolk to give to Edward, Prince of Wales (who would become King Edward VII). He demolished the old house and constructed a new palace, asking Crapper & Co. to provide all sanitary ware, plumbing and drainage. And so it was that a boy without a birth date from Yorkshire ended up chatting to royalty – admittedly about loos, but who knows what else? A company history describes how, during a tour of the works, the Prince asked Mr Crapper for a light for his cigar. 'Our founder did not smoke and so could not oblige – but from that day forward he habitually carried a gold matchbox in his pocket!' The firm would receive three further royal warrants and much other work besides, including on Westminster Abbey. Indeed, Wallace Reyburn, who in 1969 wrote *Flushed With Pride: The Story of Thomas Crapper*, a book that was hailed as a 'classic of the smallest room', reveals that Crapper made a royal blue velvet armchair lavatory for Edward VII's mistress Lily Langtry at her house in Hampstead.

By all accounts, Mr Crapper had quite the life. The company, or a revived version of it, reports this of its founder: 'He enjoyed the fruits of his labours and acquired the trappings of wealth: property, land and chattels. He and his brother George drank at the Finborough Arms, in

Kensington. Regularly, they would begin the working day in the tavern with a bottle of champagne.' And, we must assume, a visit to view the Crapper Valveless Waste Preventer.

It is from Mr Reyburn that we are given the detail that Mr Crapper died after leaving his sick bed to mend a faulty cistern. His grave is white marble, as befits a sanitary-ware pioneer, but over the years it had become blackened. Thomas Crapper & Co. restored the grave to pristine condition and a rededication ceremony was held in May 2002, attended by many, including some named Crapper. The vicar even found a Bible passage referring to a cistern.

When I visited, having avoided making a trip to Piddle or Bottom, I found the grave by walking round the large Victorian cemetery until I saw a flash of white, though it was not exactly gleaming, the weather once again having taken its toll. (If you visit, walk up the main path until you see a cross with MOTHER on it, an anchor swung over it, turn right, follow the path until the end, then turn right again.) Still, Mr Crapper stands out among the grey Victorian angels and gloomy urns. There is a plaque on the front: 'Thomas Crapper: inventor and sanitary pioneer'. And, I might add, a legend in his own loo-time.

# CROSS BONES GRAVEYARD

## 1525–1853
*18–22 Redcross Way, London SE1*

If you walk south from ultra-chic Borough Market, leaving behind the frozen yoghurt at £4 a scoop and the gorgeously arranged vegetables too beautiful to buy, you will come to Redcross Way and what seems to be a derelict building site. 'Door of the Dead', says the graffiti on the metal door that is next to a metal grill fence that has been transformed into a shrine by way of a thousand ribbons, CDs, poems, macramé, baskets, dolls, cut-up lace, feathers, ropes, flowers and who knows what else. On the 'Door of the Dead', inside a graffiti heart, is scrawled 'Touch 4 Love'. You can touch for love all you want but what you cannot do is enter this door of the dead for it is chained shut.

This is Cross Bones Graveyard, part pagan shrine, part Christian memorial, on a scruffy bit of London that I would describe as a no-man's land though, in this case, it would be no-woman's land. This has been a burial ground since at least 1525 when John Stow's *Survey of London* referred to it in this passage as the 'Single Woman's Churchyard':

> I have heard of ancient men, of good credit, report that these single women were forbidden the rites of the church, so long as they continued that sinful life, and were excluded from Christian burial, if they were not reconciled before their death. And therefore there was a plot of ground called the Single Woman's Churchyard, appointed for them far from the parish church.

In the middle of the shrine, hanging on the fence, is a plaque that depicts a goose walking across it. The text says:

'In medieval times there was an unconsecrated graveyard for prostitutes or "Winchester Geese". By the eighteenth century it had become a paupers' burial ground which closed in 1853. Here local people have created a memorial shrine.' It ends with this: 'The Outcast Dead R.I.P.'

I have to tell you that this place feels a bit wild, edgy and eerie. One statement on the grill pays tribute to the 'Wild Feminine' which is defined as 'whore and virgin, mother and lover, maiden and crone, creator and destroyer'. Locals gather on the 23rd of every month to honour the ancestors and spirit of the place. Every Halloween there is a larger gathering to pay tribute to those who lie underneath, London's forgotten people: the prostitutes, the poor, the children, the outcasts. All events seem to involve gin.

In centuries past, London was a tale of two cities split by the Thames. North of the river lay the churches and monasteries, the guilds and places of learning. And South? It was called 'The Liberty' because it was beyond the legal reach of the City. Here, anything went – brothels, bear-baiting, theatres, taverns. It was all licensed by the Bishop of Winchester (which is why prostitutes were called 'Winchester geese'). The church was happy to accept their money but not their bodies and so, at death, they were buried in shallow graves without fanfare. As the decades, then centuries, piled up at Cross Bones, so did the bodies. In the 1990s, during the Jubilee Line extension, archaeological digs revealed there to be an estimated 15,000 bodies here, a third of which were infants. The discoveries inspired a local 'shaman' and author John Constable to write a series of poems and plays called *The Southwark Mysteries* and this, in turn, inspired the first Halloween gathering.

I feel it cannot be long before academics start to study what is taking place at Cross Bones, the way that this place of the dispossessed is being possessed by local people and campaigners. It is a place of pilgrimage for many still, for prostitutes, pagans, spirits of all kinds, not to mention the just plain curious. If you peer through the grill, you will see a little garden with a statue of the Madonna. The site is owned by London Underground. This part of London is becoming achingly trendy but there is a powerful campaign to remember Cross Bones in some way, perhaps as a memorial garden, so the Outcast Dead really can, finally, RIP.

## WILLIAM GILBERT GRACE

### CRICKETER
### 18 July 1848–23 October 1915
*Beckenham Cemetery, Elmers End Road, Beckenham, Kent BR3 4TD*

His grave is gleaming white, which seems about right, for it would never do for the man whom many believe was the greatest cricketer that ever lived to have a dreary grey stone, like those that surround his. Actually, it is even better than that in that it is a white cross monument with a bed that is filled with stones as green as the grass on a cricket pitch. It is a family grave, for him and his wife, and two of their four children. In the middle of the 'grass', there is a plaque with a small drawing of a bat and wicket with this inscription: 'W. G. Grace, Doctor and Cricketer'.

He was much more the latter than the former. He was born in Downend near Bristol (he spoke with a Gloucester accent throughout his life), into a family of nine, all of whom played cricket almost from birth. His father was a doctor and W. G., as he was called even from a young age, followed that career only because it was expected of him. He did not qualify, working around cricketing commitments, until the age of thirty-one. Geoffrey Moorhouse, in *Wisden Cricketers' Almanack* in 1988, remarked that, other than being a supremely talented cricketer, there wasn't that much else to the man, other than devotion to his family.

A hand of whist appears to have marked the limit of his capacity for cerebration, and if one wished to be rude to suburbia one might identify Grace as suburban man incarnate, fluctuating mentally as well as physically between the fringes of Bristol and the London Counties, ultimately coming to rest in Eltham. His one inherited asset was that he came from a clan which was dotty about a great game and dutiful (in some cases no more) about the general practice of medicine, with no doubt in its collective mind which came first at all times and in all places. His brother E. M. Grace, who was a coroner, once had a corpse put on ice until he could attend to it at close of play.

A suburban man who has ended up, then, in suburbia, for what else could Beckenham (near Eltham) be called. After he retired from first-class cricket, he continued to play for Eltham, playing his very last game at sixty-six, just after the outbreak of the First World War. The *Times* obituary of him notes that he succeeded in being a legend in his own lifetime, a man who was attributed deeds that he had never, in fact, done. But, truly, does it matter when the deeds he *had* done include scoring more than 54,000 first-class runs over forty-four seasons, including 389 in just eight days in 1876, when he hit several triple centuries? *The Times*, when he died, head-lined his obituary THE WORLD'S GREATEST CRICKETER. But, for some, like Moorhouse, he is not a hero, because of his ruthless competitive streak and his acute eye for the money-making opportunity, ironic given his celebrated amateur status.

He was one of those men whose very appearance – tall, heavy, bushy beard, lumbering carriage, bright yellow and red cap – can be instantly conjured up even by people who know very little about the game. As Sir Ian Botham has noted, 'He was like the father figure of cricket. He was the first superstar of the game.' On the day of Grace's funeral, Sir Arthur Conan Doyle wrote an appreciation of the great man in *The Times*. This, then, gives you a taste of W. G:

His style and methods were peculiar to himself. In his youth, when he was tall, slim and agile, he must have been as ideal in his form as in his results. But as this generation knew him, he had run to great size and a certain awkwardness of build. As he came towards the wicket, walking heavily with shoulders rounded, his great girth outlined by his coloured sash, one would have imagined that his day was past. He seemed slow, stiff, and heavy at first. When he had made 50 in his quiet methodical fashion, he was somewhat younger and fresher. At the end of a century, he had not turned a hair and was watching the ball with as clear an eye as in the first over. It was his advice to play every ball as if it were the first – and he lived up to it.

Sir Arthur ends with this: 'Those who knew him will never look at the classic sward of Lord's without an occasional vision of the great cricketer.' But I don't think it's only those who knew him who can conjure up an image of W. G. Grace. It is even possible to do so in deeply suburban Beckenham.

## MAHOMET WEYONOMON

### NATIVE AMERICAN CHIEF
**Birth unknown–died 1736**
*Southwark Cathedral, London Bridge, London SE1 9DA*

The tombstone is a strange sight: a bit like a lop-sided anthill, a pink granite mound with parallel lines flowing across and around. It's right in the middle of the action, just across from London Bridge station in the grounds of Southwark Cathedral, abutting the exuberant food stalls of Borough Market. A grave marker says: 'Mahomet Weyonomon, Sachem of the Mohegans of Connecticut was buried in this churchyard 1736.' I discover from a plaque nearby that Sachem means chief. The grave is in the middle of a plot of balding grass, next to its very own snack kiosk. Music from the market – 'Get Ready' by The Temptations – provides a soundtrack. Actually, the whole place is swarming, exactly like an anthill, as people, mostly tourists, walk by or sit to chow down on lunch. Mahomet, forgotten for 270 years, will never now be lonely.

The cathedral has many American connections (the founder of Harvard was baptised here and has a chapel inside) but I doubt it has ever seen the likes of Mahomet's grave dedication ceremony in November 2006. The Queen and Prince Philip attended, along with the American ambassador, the Dean of Southwark and Mohegan tribal leaders in deerskin leggings, breechcloths and headdresses bristling with turkey and eagle feathers. 'We cannot right past wrongs but we can remember them and transform them to inspire better conduct throughout humanity now and in years to come,' said the Very Rev. Colin Slee, Dean of Southwark, during the service.

The past wrongs date from the early 1700s when English settlers came to the east coast of America and, specifically, the area that is now south-central Connecticut. Mohegan, translated from the Algonquin dialect, the Mohegan-Pequot language, means People of the Wolf. Relations between the tribe and the settlers were, on the face of it, friendly, but the English kept encroaching on the Mohegan land. By 1735, according to the letter carried across the Atlantic by Mahomet, his tribe's land had been reduced to 'less than two miles square out of the large territories for their hunting and planting'.

The idea of Mahomet's trip was to petition King George II for help in regaining what was rightfully theirs. He was accompanied by two settlers who supported his cause and another Mohegan. They took lodgings in the City, and waited. The King referred the case to a commission. They waited some more. In the end, Mahomet would die waiting, having caught smallpox. As a foreigner he could not be buried in the City of London and so, or at least as the myth tells us, his body was taken by torch-lit boat across the river and placed in an unmarked grave. Back home, following the failure of the mission, the tribe lost even more ground to what was then the colony of Connecticut. It wasn't until

1994 that the Mohegans were given a reservation by the federal government.

'He didn't have a proper funeral in our tribal tradition,' said Mohegan spiritual leader Bruce 'Two Dogs' Bozsum of Uncasville, which is a town on the reservation. 'This is what we want to give him now.'

Two Dogs approached the cathedral, and the dean and sculptor Peter Randall Page flew out to Uncasville to choose a hunk of pink granite, in line with the custom of naming a boulder after a chief who dies. The grooves in the resulting sculpture represent trails. After the memorial service at the cathedral, during which the words of the petition were read out and Prince Philip read from *The Letter to the Hebrews*, the exotic-looking group moved outside, where Two Dogs conducted a 'smudge blessing' with songs and prayers, also burning sage and tobacco in a clam shell. 'We capture the smoke in our left hands, pull it over our hearts and say a prayer as we release it up to the Creator,' explained Two Dogs. He said that Mahomet had brought a stone peace pipe to give to King George II. Now Queen Elizabeth accepted a similar gift and finally, after all this time, the petition was put into the hand of royalty. 'Mahomet has his stone now,' said Two Dogs. 'And his place in history.'

# FREDERICK YORK WOLSELEY

## INVENTOR AND SHEEP SHEARER
### 16 March 1837–8 January 1899
*Beckenham Cemetery, Elmers End Road,*
*Beckenham, Kent BR3 4TD*

I happened upon Fred, as he was known, while looking for the grave of W. G. Grace. He has a shiny, black granite headstone that says: 'Inventor of the sheep shearing machine in Australia and producer of the first British motor car in England.' Even those of us who may have become a little blasé about the tendency for epitaphs to emphasise the extraordinaire had to stop for this one. What a combo. I had to know more. A clue was provided by the stone which said that it had been erected in 1988 for the Australian bicentennial by Wolseley enthusiasts worldwide.

So, first, the sheep which, indeed, were first for Fred. Born in Ireland, he went to New South Wales at the age of seventeen to be a jackaroo. The exact location, which I know because there is now a monument there to mark the spot, is in Wakool Road in (yes) Wakool. It says:

> This cairn marks the locality of Cobran homestead, where a 17-year-old Irishman named Frederick York Wolseley gained his five years 'colonial experience'. He lived on Cobran and Thule for twenty-two years. It was here he dreamed of creating a mechanical method of shearing sheep and in time perfected the machine that bore his name. This has become part of the rich history of the wool industry and is now perpetuated in poem and song.

Sadly, I could find no poems or songs but I did find a picture of the steam-powered Wolseley Portable Shearing Machine, which looks as if it was invented by Jack Robinson to my inexperienced-in-sheep eye. This was the end result, in 1887, of a series of experiments that began in 1872. Along the way, Fred bought various patents, including that of the John Howard horse clipper. And, unlike so many inventions, this one really did change the world. For more than 4,000 years, shearers removed wood from sheep by hand, using scissor-like blades. No longer.

In 1887, a young engineer named Herbert Austin joined the Wolseley Sheep Shearing Machine Company in Australia and, five years later, he and Fred headed to Birmingham to open a factory there. Demand for sheep shearing machines was seasonal and, during down periods, they made bicycles. I am sure you have guessed what is coming next, for in the 1890s Austin turned his engineering talents to making a car, which he named The Wolseley. It is not clear, other than the company link, what Fred himself had to do with the car business. Handsome and likeable, Fred may have had to hire in engineering talent but he did possess the one thing that all successful inventors require: perseverance.

Fred, who resigned as managing editor in 1894, had cancer for the last ten years of his life and died in Penge in 1899, aged sixty-two. The grave of the man whose machine transformed Australia's rural economy and facilitated the British motor car was unmarked for nearly ninety years. During that time, however, his name had a life of its own. First there was the sheep-shearing company which still exists today, now as a major supplier of building products in the UK. Then there is the name of the car which is, of course, a classic. And you may have heard of the Wolseley restaurant in Piccadilly, the *bistro du jour* for everyone who is anyone (if you want to see Hollywood in London, there are worse places to look). It carries his name because that was the site of the Wolseley car showroom, built in 1920, its grand, vaulted interior inspired by Venice and Florence.

So that is Fred's story. The next time you see the name Wolseley, you know where it comes from.

*Daniel Lambert, Saint Martin's Church, Stamford, Lincolnshire*

# ENGLAND
## EAST

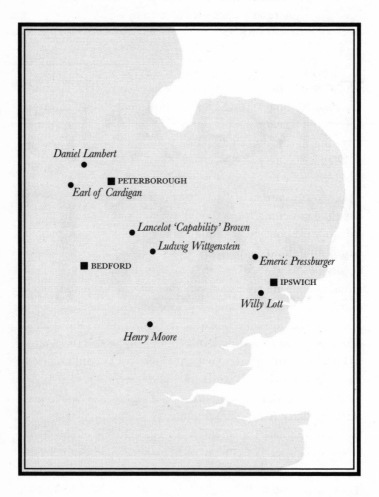

# LANCELOT 'CAPABILITY' BROWN

## LANDSCAPE GARDENER
### August 1716–6 February 1783
*St Peter and St Paul's Church, Fenstanton,
Cambridgeshire PE28 9JL*

The only thing you can say when you see Capability Brown's final resting place is: 'Oh dear'. Here is a man known for creating wide, green, undulating lawns, awe-inspiring vistas, romantic forests that would part at just the right place to reveal a classical temple or statue. He never allowed a little thing like Nature to stand in his way. When he designed the garden at Chatsworth, he decided that nothing less than widening the River Derwent would do. His whole life story is about overcoming barriers: he was born poor in Northumberland, working his way up from gardener's boy to become *the* landscape architect to Britain's aristocracy in the 1700s, pioneering a romantic and (ruthlessly) naturalistic style that would literally change the face of England. Surely he deserves a tomb site as dramatic as his horizons? But instead he ended up *inside* a church in Fenstanton, just off the A14.

There is nothing wrong with St Peter and St Paul's Church (or its graveyard), which is surrounded by houses and a car park, but Arcadia it isn't. So how did he end up here? After all, Capability (who got his name by telling his clients that their gardens had 'capabilities') lived in London, in Hampton Court to be specific, as he worked for the King. But it seems that in 1767, the Lord of Northampton owed him £12,000 (vistas don't come cheap) and he gave Capability the Manor of Fenstanton instead. I am not sure how much time the famously hyperactive Capability actually spent lording it up there, but when he died in London on 6 February, his body was brought to Fenstanton. His tomb, marble, crenulated like

a crown, includes a centre panel with a stanza in red lettering
that begins:

> YE SONS OF ELEGANCE WHO TRULY TASTE
> THE SIMPLE CHARMS THAT GENUINE ART SUPPLIES,
> COME FROM SYLVAN SCENES IS GENIUS GRAC'D
> AND OFFER HERE YOUR TRIBUTARY SIGH'S

I won't go on. It all seems alarmingly fussy. He also has a
relatively new tombstone outside the church which says that
he is buried nearby. It looks out over the graveyard, into a
suburban scene that lacks quite a lot including, it must be
said, capabilities.

# 7ᵀᴴ EARL OF CARDIGAN, JAMES THOMAS BRUDENELL

## SOLDIER
### 16 October 1797–28 March 1868
*St Peter's Church, Deene, Corby, Northamptonshire NN17 3EJ*

If you want to know about the 7ᵗʰ Earl of Cardigan, you could do worse than to read the views of one Harry Flashman, the great cad hero created by novelist George MacDonald Fraser. This is what he had to say about the man in his first book:

> You have heard all about him, no doubt. The regimental scandals, the Charge of the Light Brigade, the vanity, stupidity, and extravagance of the man – these things are history. Like most history they have a fair basis in fact. But I knew him, probably as few other officers knew him, and in turn I found him amusing, frightening, vindictive, charming and downright dangerous. He was God's own original fool – there's no doubt of that – although he was not to blame for the fiasco at Balaclava; that was Raglan and Airey between them. And he was arrogant as no other man could be, even when his wrongheadedness was there for all to see. That was his great point, the key to his character: he could never be wrong.

Indeed, the Earl of Cardigan, who never had doubts about casting himself in the role of the hero, seems to have been all of the above and so much more. He was an aristocrat who, by virtue of birth, inherited wealth and his position in society, was able to buy his place in the military, his place in Parliament and live in tranquil splendour in the lovely Deene Park in Northamptonshire with his second wife, Agnes de Horsey, who put up with his affairs and had been, herself, his mistress as his first wife lay dying.

His tomb, inside St Peter's Church, next to Deene Park, reflects the man rather well, I suspect, in that it is stonkingly vainglorious. The earl, in splendid white marble, lies facing upwards, his boots on, uniform pressed for perpetuity, sword clasped to his cold chest, mutton chops fearsome even in death. There is no sign here of the vest he wore to keep warm in the Crimea, now immortalised in the eponymous jumper beloved of old men with pipes. His wife Agnes is next to him, skirts almost as voluminous as his facial hair, face turned to him. These sculptures, by J. E. Boehm, the man who also created the Duke of Wellington at Hyde Park Corner, lie atop a green and pink marble sarcophagus, decorated with scenes from the Crimean War. Winged horses anchor the corners: the earl was an accomplished horseman and his horse, Ronald, which he rode during the Battle of Balaclava, lives on, in a way, with his stuffed head mounted and on show in the great house that is next to the churchyard.

The earl is surrounded by his ancestors, who date back to the 1500s, and is bathed in light from a stained glass window. It was absolutely freezing on the day that I visited but that, too, seemed appropriate. For here lies a vestige of a past for which few mourn. Even in death, the Earl seems to exude a cold arrogance and yet, looking at him, you cannot help but shake your head in wonder at those days. The church is no longer in use (you will need to get the key for it from the Deene Park office) and is cared for by the Churches Conservation Trust. This too seems appropriate. This is not a living place and I see from the signs in the Brudenell chapel that the bats have moved in. Still, I loved it.

# WILLY LOTT

## FARM WORKER
### 1761 (date unknown)–12 July 1849
*St Mary the Virgin Churchyard, The Street, East Bergholt,*
*Suffolk CO7 6TA*

# JOHN CONSTABLE

## PAINTER
### 11 June 1776–31 March 1837
*St John-at-Hampstead Churchyard, Church Row,*
*London NW3 6UU*

Willy Lott was king of the staycation. 'Sacred to the memory of William Lott,' says his gravestone, 'who departed this life at 88 years, resided at Gibeons Farm, near Flatford Mill, in this parish all his life'. According to legend, in all those years, the tenant farmer only spent four nights away from home.

As I stood, reading the gravestone, a man in a Barbour jacket with a small dog on a lead strode by on the path through the churchyard at picturesque East Bergholt. 'Ah, visiting Willy Lott, are you?' he said, though it wasn't really a question. I get the feeling that many do. Indeed, a few hours later, after we'd visited Willy Lott's cottage at Flatford Mill, now owned by the National Trust, we drove by the church and saw someone else at Willy's grave.

This is the epicentre of Constable Country, as it is now called. John Constable was born and grew up here, solidly middle class, son of a corn merchant, in a house that is no more but was just up the road from the church. His parents are in the graveyard – on the other side of it, where there is also a bell cage, built in 1531 as a temporary measure. It's still there. But East Bergholt is that kind of place. Solid. Quiet. Unfashionable. I imagine that, at its core, it hasn't changed all that much since Willy and John lived here, not a mile from each other. John's father actually owned Flatford Mill where, of course, Willy was born. We know nothing much about Willy but, then, it is only because of John that we know of him at all.

It almost never happened. John was supposed to go into his father's business and it took until 1799, when he was twenty-three, to convince his parents that he should become a painter. He'd grown up sketching the landscape around East Bergholt and, after he moved to London where he painted portraits ('dull') to pay the bills, he still returned most summers to paint the everyday scenes of country life. His love of nature and his desire to capture it – the sky, the trees, the water, exactly as it was – was revolutionary at the time. Married to a childhood friend, Maria, they had seven children. In his lifetime, he sold just twenty paintings in England and wasn't elected to the Royal Academy until he was fifty-two. Constable wasn't exactly a failure but neither could he be called a success. Hopeless with money, happy in love, he cuts a romantic figure, painting his clouds over Hampstead and his Willy Lott scenes.

The cottage looks remarkably as it did when Constable painted it as part of *The Hay Wain*. You can walk down to Flatford Mill and stand more or less where Constable did when he made his outdoor sketches in 1821. The painting was originally entitled 'Landscape: Noon' because he had to stop at that time, or otherwise he would be looking directly into the sun. (Sun? In England? Surely not.) When he first exhibited the painting, it didn't sell. Now *The Hay Wain* is priceless and hangs in Room 34 of the National Gallery.

Someone should write a play about the relationship

between Willy Lott and John Constable. Did the farmer ever look over the painter's shoulder? What did they talk about? Did they like each other? They certainly shared a love for the countryside and the rhythms of everyday life. 'I would rather be a poor man in England than a rich man abroad,' Constable wrote to a friend, explaining why he would not travel to promote his work. But when Maria died from TB, aged forty-one, Constable went into mourning and wore black for the rest of his life. She was buried in a raised tomb in a corner of St John's Churchyard in Hampstead. He is there with two of their children. It's a shady corner, green and tumbledown. There is no view.

'Some are born great, some have greatness thrust upon them,' says a plaque at Flatford Mill. How ironic that the tenant farmer who spent only four nights away from home in his exceptionally long life is now known around the world. I would bet that his simple gravestone receives more visitors than the much grander one in Hampstead. Constable may have been one of the greats but he needed Willy Lott more than Willy Lott needed him.

## DANIEL LAMBERT

### EXHIBITIONIST AND GAOLER
### 13 March 1770–21 June 1809
*St Martin's Church, High Street, Stamford,*
*Lincolnshire PE9 2LF*

EXHIBITION. – Mr. DANIEL LAMBERT, of Leicester, the
greatest Curiosity in the World, who, at the age of 36, weighs
upwards of FIFTY STONE (14lb to the stone). Mr Lambert
will see Company at his House, No.53, Piccadilly, opposite St
James's Church from 12 to 5 o'clock. – Admittance 1s.

This is the advertisement that ran in *The Times* on 2 April
1806, signalling the end of Daniel Lambert's career as a
gaol-keeper and the beginning of his life as a 'Curiosity of
the World'. The idea of displaying himself for money had
been born out of desperation, after Bridewell gaol was closed
in 1805 and he found himself without a job. Lambert was
gigantic, approaching 50 stone, with six men of normal size
being able to fit inside his waistcoat. By all accounts he was so
amazingly fat for the simple reason that he ate too much and
did too little. Everyone he met seemed to be fascinated by his
size. And so, in a way that many D-list celebrities today will
recognise, he decided to cash in on this: he placed an advert
in *The Times* and went to London, via a reinforced carriage,
to make his name.

The venture sounds a somewhat genteel version of *I'm
a Celebrity, Get Me Out of Here*, if such a thing were possible.
Lambert did his best to avoid being seen as a freak, creating
instead a sort of 'At Home' ambience, where he chatted to
his (paying) guests, not least about his expertise in field sports
and animal breeding. Affable and good-looking, he was an
immediate sensation, attracting four hundred visitors a day.

The medical world got in on the act, weighing and examining him. Cartoonists drew him. Famous dwarfs visited him. His name became slang for being fat. A copycat (and somewhat slimmer) fake Daniel Lambert set up shop nearby. The upper classes were entranced and he even met King George III.

After six months, the Curiosity of the World retired back to Leicester, a rich man who now could afford to indulge his passion for sport and dog-breeding. Once in a while, he would make short fundraising trips. Thus, in June 1809, he had set off a tour round East Anglia, ending at Stamford, where he would go to the races. At the time, Lambert weighed 52 stone 11lbs (739lbs or 335 kg). Too large to climb stairs, he found ground-floor lodgings and got himself installed (one account says his stomach looked like 'a featherbed'). Indeed he was so huge that he couldn't go to the printers and so he sent a message – 'As the Mountain could not wait upon Mahomet, Mahomet would go to the Mountain' – to come and see him to organise the handbills. But the next morning he was taken unexpectedly ill while shaving and, within minutes, died. No one knew why (though I think we can guess the root cause).

The coffin was 6ft 4in. long (he was 5ft 11) and 4ft 4in. wide. It had wheels. It sounds, from reports, as if the coffin-maker must have come to him (the Mountain, even in death, was waited upon). But to get the coffin out of the inn, a wall had to be demolished. It took twenty men to pull the coffin to the grave at St Martin's.

Today Stamford is an unexpected delight, well-preserved (even the toilets are Grade II listed) with little passages off the high street. It looks like a film set, which, at times, it has been (for *Middlemarch* and *The Da Vinci Code* apparently). Lambert is buried in what someone described to us as the 'secret grave-yard', which is just beyond the original graveyard, behind St Martin's. The grave, decorated with primroses, looks a disap-pointingly normal size, though of course, below ground, the elm coffin must still be enormous. His may be the only grave-stone in England with his vital measurements on it. It says:

> IN REMEMBRANCE OF THAT PRODIGY IN NATURE,
> DANIEL LAMBERT
> A NATIVE OF LEICESTER
> WHO WAS POSSESSED OF AN EXALTED AND CONVIVIAL MIND
> AND IN PERSONAL GREATNESS HAD NO COMPETITOR
> HE MEASURED 3FT 1IN ROUND THE LEG
> 9FT 4IN ROUND THE BODY
> AND WEIGHED 52 STONE 11 POUNDS
> HE DEPARTED ON 21 JUNE 1809
> AGED 39 YEARS

Up the road, at the George Inn, there is not so much a spectacle as a display, with an oil painting of Lambert, his extremely stout walking stick and a cartoon called 'Fat and Lean'. It shows Lambert, his chest and stomach covered in a vast expanse of stripy waistcoating, with a wraith of a woman on his (extremely cushioned) knee. They are both positioned on an orange love seat which, if real, would surely have collapsed immediately. The Curiosity of the World indeed.

# HENRY SPENCER MOORE

## SCULPTOR
### 30 July 1898–31 August 1986
*St Thomas' Graveyard, Perry Green, Much Hadham,*
*Hertfordshire SG10 6EE*

For a man who loved the monumental, Henry Moore's grave is surprisingly life-sized. In fact, it's not even a grave, only a headstone in the ground. Two headstones, actually, for he and his wife Irina lie side by side in the churchyard of St Thomas', in a little place that is no more than a hamlet really, called Perry Green. Their headstones are simple, grey, elegant, ordinary, placed in front of a blackthorn bush that was sprinkled with white blossom when I visited in early spring. This is a classic English churchyard, with its sinuous old yews, birdsong and sprinkling of wild primroses. His gravestone says: 'Henry Moore 1898–1986 Sculptor'.

Here, then, is the grave of one of the most monumental artists that Britain has ever produced. It's a fascinating place, Perry Green: so small and so English and yet home to Moore's ginormous and, in many ways, very un-English pieces. It was pure serendipity that brought him here. During the Second World War, the Moores had come to visit a friend, Leonard Matters, an MP with a strange interest in Jack the Ripper. Upon returning to their Hampstead home, they discovered it had been bombed. They went back to Perry Green and stayed there, creating a home, garden and sculpture park, which is now run by the Henry Moore Foundation.

It is here, in the landscape, and specifically a field of sheep, that you can find a proper tribute to Henry Moore. His studio, which has been kept as it was, is a fascinating hodgepodge of bones, maquettes and everyday bits and pieces. In one corner sits the monumental skull of an elephant – his favourite natural object, apparently. Next to the skull is a window that looks out on a field of sheep and it was here, when preparing for an exhibit in 1972, that he began to draw them. 'I've always been fascinated by sheep,' he said. 'No other animal quite has that ancient Biblical quality.' And fascinated also, perhaps, because they are just the right shape for him as an artist.

The sculpture park has some thirty pieces, but it is hard not to be drawn to *Sheep Piece*, its huge rounded forms – meant to symbolise mother and child, a favourite theme in Moore's work, though in this case ewe and lamb, of course – standing proud in the middle of a field of the real thing. When I was there, about a dozen sheep were rubbing against *Sheep Piece*, burnishing the metal, creating another layer of meaning, taking shelter from the rain.

At the farthest end of this field, on a rough hillock, something rises out of the land that is truly otherworldly. This is *Large Reclining Figure, 1984*, its semi-abstract alien form spread against the sky. Henry Moore not only created the sculpture but also the hill it sits on. 'When I acquired the ground it was a pyramid of waste gravel,' he said. 'But you cannot put a sculpture on a pyramid if the point is too small, so I had a bulldozer shape it into a small hill.'

The original *Large Reclining Figure*, created in 1938, was a tiny lead cast that was purchased by the Museum of Modern Art in New York. It wasn't until 1983 that Moore created a ten-metre-long enlargement for the architect I. M. Pei's Overseas Chinese Banking Corporation in Singapore. After this Moore decided that the huge form was exactly what was needed for the top of his man-made hillock. A fibreglass version was installed but the bronze version that is seen there today was not put in place until after Moore's death. For me, this sculpture is truly his monument, a piece of magic left behind, a strange pin-headed form with a sense of the arachnid about it that actually touches the sky and watches over his gravestone from on high.

## EMERIC PRESSBURGER

### FILM-MAKER
### 5 December 1902–5 February 1988
*St Mary of Grace Church, Aspall, nr Debenham, Suffolk IP14*

Emeric, born Imre in Hungary in 1902, was the Pressburger of Powell–Pressburger fame, the producer, director and writing duo behind such films as *49th Parallel* and *The Red Shoes*. As a young man Emeric moved on to Germany to work as a film script-writer in 1933. In a marvellous joint appearance on *Desert Island Discs*, he and Michael Powell told what happened next:

> Roy Plomley : Then you decided to move to France?
> Pressburger: I decided to when Hitler came.
> Powell: It was decided for you.
> Pressburger: It was decided by him.

It is fascinating to listen as they tell their stories and pick their records (Emeric's more musical for he played the violin, reportedly very well). They finish each other's sentences, phrases blurring, voices blending perfectly. They met in England in 1935, when both worked for the great Alexander Korda. This is what Emeric said of Michael: 'He knows what I am going to say even before I say it – maybe even before I have thought it – and that is very rare. You are lucky if you meet someone like that once in your life.'

In their later lives, Powell lived in Gloucestershire (where he is buried)* and Pressburger in Suffolk. He once said that a film should have a good story and also, if possible, a little bit

---

* Michael Powell, 1905–1990, is buried in Holy Cross Churchyard in Avening, Gloucestershire. His epitaph reads: 'Film director and optimist'.

of magic. 'Magic being untouchable and very difficult to cast, you can't deal with it at all. You can only try to prepare some nests, hoping that a little bit of magic will slide into them,' he said. Well, what can be true about films can also be true about gravestones.

Emeric Pressburger's grave lies in Our Lady of Grace in a tiny gathering of three or four homes in deepest Suffolk. We visit on a cold, clear February day. His stone, lying flat, is near the path that goes to the front door of the church. The inscription reads:

> LOVE RULES THE COURT, THE CAMP, THE GROVE,
> THIS WORLD BELOW AND HEAVEN ABOVE,
> FOR LOVE IS HEAVEN,
> AND HEAVEN IS LOVE.

This is from a Sir Walter Scott poem quoted in the Powell–Pressburger film *A Matter of Life and Death*. It may be the best epitaph ever. His grandson, the film director Kevin Macdonald, who wrote his biography, *The Life and Death of a Screenwriter*, described the funeral:

> It was a cold dreary day and a small funeral, a few friends from the village, the Schopflinns, my brother and I and our father. Michael was unable to come. Martin Scorsese sent flowers. At the last minute a long-forgotten Yugoslav cousin rang from Belgrade to ensure we gave our grandfather a Jewish burial. He assured us that Emeric had been a practising Jew. No one else could remember him going near a synagogue. As a concession, the liberal Anglican vicar allowed a Star of David to be engraved on his grave stone.

And indeed there it is today, a little bit of stardust in deepest Suffolk.

# LUDWIG JOSEF JOHANN WITTGENSTEIN

## PHILOSOPHER
### 26 April 1889–29 April 1951
*Ascension Parish Burial Ground, All Souls Lane,*
*Huntingdon Road, Cambridge CB3 0EA*

I am writing this on the anniversary of Ludwig Wittgenstein's death which, to me at least, feels logical. Would he think so? Who could possibly know? The great thing about Ludwig Wittgenstein is that he remains, even in death, indeed especially in death, mysterious. After all, this is a man whose earlier and later work formed the points of origin of two schools of philosophy (logical positivism and the philosophy of ordinary language), both of which he disowned. He published very little in his life and he did everything he could to prevent the circulation of his notes on the grounds that if they were read, they would be misunderstood.

His life, unlike his grave, was about as complicated as it gets. Born in Austria to a rich family, he went to Cambridge in 1912 to study under Bertrand Russell (who proclaimed him a genius) but then went back and fought for Austria in the First World War, until he became a prisoner of war in Italy. There he completed his one and only manuscript, *Tractatus Logico-Philosophicus*. In 1922, though, he gave away all his wealth and went to teach in a mountain village in Austria. By 1930, he was back at Cambridge, only to leave again to live in a mountain hut in Norway in 1936. But he was back in 1938 and succeeded G. E. Moore as Cambridge Chair of Philosophy in 1939. He then left to become a hospital porter... I won't continue. I think you get the idea. He may have been a genius but he was also, to use a technical term, a bit bonkers. Still, he was clearly adored by colleagues and friends.

His grave, in the magical Ascension Burial Ground in

Cambridge, where, incidentally, G. E. Moore also lies, gives little away. It is a slab on the ground with his (truncated) name, Ludwig Wittgenstein, and the years of his birth and death. 'That's all he wanted, plain like that,' the caretaker said in 1980. In a graveyard that includes the most extraordinary collection of brains – the combined IQ of this romantic topsy-turvy place must be astronomical – his is by far the most visited. When I was there, there were many pennies scattered round his stone. Sometimes the pennies are organised in different (supposedly logical) ways on the grave. I was also sad to have missed a miniature ladder which has often been photographed on the grave, placed there, apparently, in homage to section 6.54 of the *Tractatus*, 'My propositions are elucidatory in this way: he who understands me finally recognises them as senseless, when he has climbed out through them, on them, over them. (He must so to speak throw away the ladder, after he has climbed up on it.) He must surmount these propositions; then he sees the world rightly.' To which I think one can only say that we must all take life one rung at a time.

*Pip's Graves, St James' Church, Cooling, Kent*

# SOUTH-EAST ENGLAND

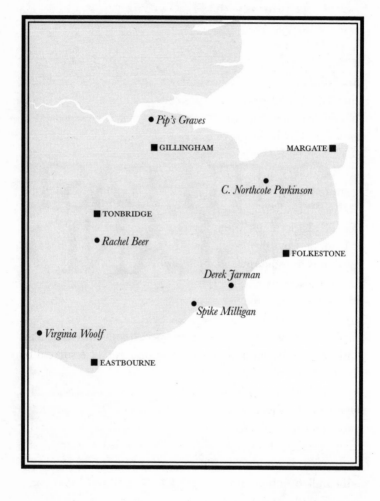

# MICHAEL DEREK ELWORTHY JARMAN

## ARTIST
### 31 January 1942–19 February 1994
*St Clement's Church, Old Romney, Kent TN29 0HP*

Derek Jarman, film-maker, Aids activist, gardener extraordinaire, is a man whose life was art. There is something ultra cool about his gravestone at St Clement's Churchyard in Old Romney. Square, thickish, and black, it stands near the edge. On it, in flowing script, is simply his signature – *Derek Jarman*. Its location, quite neatly, is part of two worlds. To one side is the gorgeous medieval St Clement's Church, surrounded by fields, sheep so real that they look painted on. To the other there is the A259, the sound of traffic, the ugliness of raggle-taggle buildings that straggle along it.

I stopped by his grave on a wintry spring day on my way to what is his real memorial – his garden at Prospect Cottage in Dungeness, which he bought in 1986, entranced by the strangeness of it all. I drove through the town of Lydd (I notice he didn't choose to be buried in that suburban churchyard) and onwards, the scenario becoming flatter, bleaker and stranger by the minute, made infinitely more surreal by the presence of a nuclear power station at the end of the road. I head over the track for the little Romney, Hythe and Dymchurch railway, whose 23-kilometre coastal journey ends here. This feels like the edge of something: if not the world, then certainly England. To my left, the shingle approach to the coast is studded with the flotsam and rubbish of fishing – the hulk of a boat out of water, sheds of all types and large, quite unfathomable (to me) arrangements of metal. To my right, there is a string of little houses, some of them hardly more than shacks. Jarman said twilight here was like nowhere else. 'You feel as you stand here that tired time is having a snooze.' This isn't hyperbole.

I recognised the cottage immediately, its tarry blackness offset by bright yellow windows. The wind was vicious (Jarman, when he came here, asked someone if the wind ever stopped). Jarman was diagnosed with Aids just after he bought the cottage, and the garden that he created here was his final masterpiece. It surrounds the house: it is sculptural, circular, made of driftwood, stones, flint, indigenous plants, and others that he introduced. 'Paradise haunts gardens and some gardens are paradises. Mine is one of them,' he said. On the side of the house, filling half of the wall, in black letters, there a poem from John Donne's *The Sun Rising,* which ends:

> Shine here to us, and thou art everywhere;
> This bed thy centre is, these walls thy sphere.

It is a private house, so I stayed across the road, looking, but it was enough.

## PIP'S GRAVES

### 1767–1854
*St James' Church, Main Road, Cooling,*
*nr Rochester, Kent ME3 8DG*

'Ours was the marsh country, down by the river, within, as the river wound, twenty miles of the sea...' Thus begins the first page of *Great Expectations* with young Pip in a graveyard, looking at the graves of his parents and, alongside, those of the brothers he never knew. 'Five little stone lozenges, each about a foot and a half long, which were arranged in a neat row beside their grave, and were sacred to the memory of five little brothers of mine.'

It is a long, slow snake of a drive to Cooling churchyard on the Hoo peninsula where St James' Church sits, proud, beautiful, if no longer used. I visited on a hot and sunny morning, the trees that surround the graveyard dappling the soft, green grass. But, as you look across the flatness towards the Thames estuary, the view far more industrial than in Dickens's day, it is easy to imagine how eerie this place could be: overgrown with nettles, the tombs listing, the gravestones old even then, with Pip being terrorised by the escaped convict Magwitch.

They are called, far and wide, Pip's Graves. By the church entrance the little lozenges line up around one central stone – thirteen in all, three on one side and ten on the other. All these children, from two local families, died in infancy, their dates from 1767 to 1854. All would have existed when Dickens, who lived nearby, wrote his great novel in 1861. The headstones are illegible now but you still feel that you know something of their stories. As Pip noted, looking at the graves: 'I am indebted for a belief I religiously entertained that they had all been born on their backs with their hands in their trouser pockets and had never taken them out of this state of existence.'

# TERENCE ALAN PATRICK SEÁN 'SPIKE' MILLIGAN

## COMEDIAN
### 16 April 1918–27 February 2002
*St Thomas' Church, Winchelsea, East Sussex TN36 4EB*

It was easy to find Spike Milligan's grave, for a matted grass pathway has developed, like a sheep trail but this would be a people trail, to the Celtic cross marker that stands in the windswept old graveyard that surrounds the imposing St Thomas' Church at Winchelsea. It is a Grade I listed affair, a huge building that, judging from the ruined piers attached to it, used to be even larger. It looks magnificent if just a bit comical. But then that would be natural for anything to do with Spike.

Winchelsea is almost as far as you can go in England without being in France. The day I was there was bitterly cold, with a fierce wind, and even the snowdrops cowering. I was joined by two men, one pushing a pram, who had come to pay homage to the great man. Frankly, I was pleased to see the gravestone at all as it had recently been removed, the source of a family wrangle as to whether it should be altered after the death of his third wife, Shelagh. Apparently one of his children had objected to this but now her name is there for all to see.

This is the grave that contains what is, according to a 2012 survey by Marie Curie Cancer Care, the nation's favourite epitaph: 'I told you I was ill…' This beat Oscar Wilde's quip, 'Either those curtains go or I do', and Frank Sinatra's 'The best is yet to come'. And, of course, it has the added attraction of actually existing in the UK (Wilde died in Paris, Sinatra in California). It's quite the crowded gravestone which begins with 'love, light, peace' and describes the Goon star as 'writer, artist, musician, humanitarian, comedian'. His children are listed and there is a reference to his grandchildren.

But where was the epitaph? 'He took out Irish citizenship in later years,' explained the man with the pram. According to reports, church authorities objected to the original words and so, in the best English tradition, a compromise, not to say fudge, was agreed upon. Thus I could see the words 'dúirt mé leat go raibh mé breoite'. These, I am told, are Gaelic for 'I told you I was ill'. Though, to be honest, I wouldn't bet my life on it.

# C. NORTHCOTE PARKINSON

## HISTORIAN AND WRITER
### 30 July 1909–9 March 1993
*Canterbury City Cemetery, Westgate Court*
*Avenue, Canterbury CT2 8JL*

The first time I went to find Parkinson's grave, I failed. I walked the paths of Canterbury City Cemetery. I found others. There was Joseph Conrad or, to give him his real name, Józef Teodor Konrad Korzeniowski with his epitaph from Spenser: 'Sleep after toyle, port after stormie seas, ease after warre, death after life, does greatly please.' There were soldiers, professors, doctors, lawyers, children … but where was Cyril Northcote Parkinson? I would have to return even though my graves book did have, quite appropriately, a deadline.

Still, it seemed to fit. Cyril, or C, as I think of him, may have been a distinguished naval historian who wrote dozens of books on the subject and would have appreciated Spenser's 'stormie seas'. But that is not why I was walking in circles around Canterbury Cemetery. It was because, in November 1955, in response to the publication of a royal commission report on the civil service, an article offering an insight into how work works appeared in *The Economist*, written anonymously, as is usual for that magazine:

> It is a commonplace observation that work expands so as to fill the time available for its completion. Thus, an elderly lady of leisure can spend the entire day in writing and despatching a postcard to her niece at Bognor Regis. An hour will be spent in finding the postcard, another in hunting for spectacles, half an hour in a search for the address, an hour and a quarter in composition, and twenty minutes in deciding whether or not

to take an umbrella when going to the pillar-box in the next street. The total effort which would occupy a busy man for three minutes all told may in this fashion leave another person prostrate after a day of doubt, anxiety and toil.

The correspondent continued to explain that, because work is elastic and depends on time, rather than actual volume, there is no relationship between the amount of work done and how many people do it. So the civil service may grow but that does not mean the workload has done so accordingly. 'Before the discovery of a new scientific law – herewith presented to the public for the first time, and to be called Parkinson's Law* – there has, however, been insufficient recognition of the implications of this fact in the field of public administration.' You will note the asterisk. At the bottom of the article, the asterisk was explained: *Why? Why not? – Editor.

And so Parkinson's Law was born and here I was, decades later, trailing around this cemetery, looking for a gravestone that says 'Author of Parkinson's Law' while at the same time fulfilling its prediction. Quite infuriating. And yet, of course, true. But that is the beauty of this witty, wry man's genius observation of how bureaucracies work, much of which was based on his experience working for the War Office during the Second World War.

Before Parkinson's Law, he was simply Professor Parkinson. He wrote the article while living in Singapore, having become the Raffles Professor of History at the new University of Malaya in 1950. He would continue to publish what he called 'proper work' – history, in one form or the other – while also starting a new career as satirist and soothsayer. In 1957, still in Singapore, he expanded on his *Economist* essay in the 120-page book, *Parkinson's Law*, with illustrations by Osbert Lancaster. It was an instant bestseller. Particularly brilliant is his second most famous observation, Parkinson's Law of

Triviality, which explains why a finance committee will spend two and a half minutes waving through the millions required to build a nuclear reactor, forty-five minutes on the $2,350 to build a new bike shed but one hour and fifteen minutes on the huge decision whether to spend $57 a year on refreshment for the committee. Admit it, we've all been there in one way or another, hardly noticing our mortgage while haggling over the price of one can of tuna as compared to another.

C's life – and earnings – expanded to fill the time available. Unassuming and hugely amused by the turn his life had taken, he became a celebrity and a regular on the lecture and after-dinner speaking circuits. He continued to write history as well as such books as *Parkinsanities* and *Mrs Parkinson's Law: and Other Studies in Domestic Science*. In his eighties, he moved to Canterbury with his third wife, and wrote. His obituary in *The Independent* reveals that it was with delight that he used to report what Enoch Powell had said about him: 'He's like a man who found an oil well in his back garden.'

And so, inevitably, fulfilling his dictum, I returned to the cemetery, armed with a photograph of the grave from which I could discern the background. I walked through the large main cemetery, beyond the small, perfectly manicured plot of war graves and up into an area of XH. There, four rows from the back, I found him on a black slab. Prof. Cyril Northcote Parkinson, it said, author of Parkinson's Law. 'Work expands so as to fill the time available for its completion.' And so it was expanding for me. I took a photograph. It was time to go. My deadline loomed.

# ADELINE VIRGINIA WOOLF

## NOVELIST
### 25 January 1882–28 March 1941
*Monk's House Garden, The Street, Rodmell,
Lewes, East Sussex BN7 3HF*

Back from a good weekend at Rodmell – a weekend of no
talking, sinking at once into deep safe book reading; and then
to sleep: with the May tree like a breaking wave outside & all
the garden green tunnels, mounds of green; & then to wake
into the hot still day, & never a person to be seen, never an
interruption: the place to ourselves: the long hours.
Virginia Woolf, *Diary*, Monday 13 June 1932

It is not particularly easy to get to Rodmell, a small village
on a twisty road between Lewes and the south coast. You
can walk there, if you'd like a hike, or drive, but it's not on
the way to anywhere. Virginia and Leonard Woolf bought
Monk's House at auction in 1919 for £700. 'That will be our
address for ever and ever,' Virginia declared. And she was
right. For she is still here, her spirit imbuing the house, her
ashes buried in her gorgeous blowsy garden.

Monk's House is owned by the National Trust now but it
has not been commercialised or colonised. To visit is to step
back in time, the house low and intimate, her bedroom as it
was, every object made special by some sort of decoration,
her fireplace painted by her sister Vanessa Bell. Even the air
you breathe here is Bloomsbury. Beyond the house, in the
hut where she wrote, her blue writing paper still lies there,
expectant. There are boxes filled with windfall apples and
even a set of bowls, which anyone can use. To stand in the
garden and look out over the sheep and the South Downs is
deeply satisfying.

It was from here that, on a cold March day in 1941, Virginia set off for one of her walks, exhausted and depressed after finishing her book *Between the Acts*. Her husband Leonard went to the hut to call Virginia for lunch at 12.30 and found a note, written at twelve. 'Dearest,' she wrote, 'I feel certain that I am going mad again. I feel we can't go through another of those terrible times…' Leonard immediately raised the alarm, rushing with others to the river Ouse, where it was her habit to walk. But they could not find her. Indeed, her body was not discovered for more than two weeks. She had filled her gumboots with stones.

Her ashes were buried under an elm in the garden. The elm is no more but there is a sweeping fig. On a low wall, under the branches, is Stephen Tomlin's 1931 bust of Virginia. At the other end of the wall is a bust of Leonard, made by Charlotte Hewer in 1968. Below the bust are his dates (1880–1969) and his words:

I BELIEVE PROFOUNDLY IN TWO RULES: JUSTICE AND MERCY –

THEY SEEM TO ME THE FOUNDATION
OF ALL CIVILISED LIFE AND SOCIETY

IF YOU INCLUDE UNDER MERCY TOLERATION.

On Virginia's plaque, after her dates, are these words:

DEATH IS THE ENEMY. AGAINST YOU

I WILL FLING MYSELF, UNVANQUISHED AND UNYIELDING

O DEATH!

THE WAVES BROKE ON THE SHORE.

This is from her novel *The Waves,* and the full passage includes these words: 'It is death against whom I ride with my spear crouched and my hair flying back like a young man's, like Percival's, when he galloped in India. I strike spurs into my horse.'

What spirit! And, despite what you would suppose, there is no sadness here, only stillness.

## RACHEL BEER (NÉE SASSOON)

### 7 April 1858–29 April 1927
*Kent and Sussex Cemetery, Benhall Mill Road,*
*Royal Tunbridge Wells TN2 5JJ*

For her story, see Julius
Beer in London: North
and West of the Thames.

*Jane Austen, Winchester Cathedral, Hampshire*

# SOUTH–WEST ENGLAND

Cassandra Austen●

SALISBURY ■                    ● Jane Austen

Florence Nightingale
●                    PETERSFIELD ■

Sir Arthur Conan Doyle ●        ■ SOUTHAMPTON

PORTSMOUTH ■

●Thomas Hardy        ● Mary Wollstonecraft Shelley,
Mary Wollstonecraft

■WEYMOUTH        ■ SWANAGE

# JANE AUSTEN

## WRITER
### 16 December 1775–18 July 1817
*Winchester Cathedral, The Close, Winchester,*
*Hampshire SO23 9LS*

# CASSANDRA ELIZABETH AUSTEN

## SISTER
### 9 January 1773–22 March 1845
*St Nicholas Churchyard, Chawton, Hampshire GU34 1SJ*

It is a truth, universally acknowledged, that no one really knows how Jane Austen managed to secure a burial in Winchester Cathedral: so grand, so beautiful, so full of the bones of the great and the good, not to mention saints. But here too lies Jane, then an obscure spinster who lived quietly in the nearby village of Chawton with her mother and sister, both named Cassandra. Her father, the Reverend George Austen, had died in 1805 and was buried in St Swithin's churchyard in Bath.

She'd come to Winchester with her sister in late May 1817 to be nearer her doctor. She was forty-one and no one knew exactly what she had: it is thought to have been Addison's Disease though maybe, also, some type of cancer. They'd taken lodgings at 8 College Street, a house just outside the city wall. It is now a private home, painted canary yellow, and as I stood outside, looking up, it was easy to imagine that, in the bay window on the first floor, I could see a woman with a roundish face, wearing an empire dress, a little bonnet, looking out. She held a quill pen in her hand and, because I am in charge of this fantasy, she was writing, maybe a letter or a poem. (The person whom I actually saw appeared to be wearing a hoodie: God knows what Jane would have to say about that.)

She died at 4 a.m. on Friday 18 July 1817. A few days afterwards, her sister Cassandra wrote to her niece: 'I have lost a treasure, such a Sister, such a friend as never can have been surpassed, – she was the sun of my life, the gilder of every pleasure, the soother of every sorrow.' She adds: 'The last sad ceremony is to take place on Thursday morning, her dear remains are to be deposited in the Cathedral – it is a satisfaction to me to think that they are to lie in a Building she admired so much – her precious soul I presume to hope reposes in a far superior Mansion.'

But how did Jane get such a piece of prime real estate, as the many Americans who now flock to see her here would say? It remains a mystery, though of course if she were to write the novel, I think the answer would have to be: connections. Her father was a vicar and her brother Henry had just been examined for ordination by the Bishop of Winchester. Crucially, Jane also knew the dean who would, according to a booklet written by expert Michael Wheeler, have regarded the floor of the cathedral as his freehold. And so, somehow, some way, it was decided she would lie buried there.

In 1817, women did not go to funerals and so Cassandra could not attend. The funeral was held early in the morning and attended by three of her brothers and a nephew. Her epitaph isn't short:

> The benevolence of her heart, the sweetness of her temper,
> and the extraordinary endowments of her mind obtained
> the regard of all who knew her, and the warmest love of her

intimate connections. Their grief is in proportion to their affection, they know their loss to be irreparable, but in their deepest affliction they are consoled by a firm though humble hope that her charity, devotion, faith and purity have rendered her soul acceptable in the sight of her REDEEMER.

Have you spotted the missing word? Yes, that would be 'writer'. Of course, in those days Jane would have published only under the name 'A Lady'. Personally, I think that the fact it doesn't say writer is perfect for an author who always lets readers discern the truth, gradually, by deduction. Anyway, it was set right in 1870 by a brass plaque on the wall next to the grave, paid for with proceeds from the biography written by her nephew, the Reverend James Edward Austen-Leigh. It says that she was 'known to many by her writings', which is one way of putting it. There was a bouquet beneath the plaque when we visited (and our guide said that fans often do send flowers). There is a large and beautiful memorial window above, paid for by public subscription in 1900.

But our story does not end there. For had things turned out differently, had Jane not been ill, had she finished the novel *Sanditon*, which she was in the middle of, and carried on writing many more, had she lived to the same age as Cassandra, an amateur painter whose sketches and letters provide us with so much of what we know of Jane, which was seventy-two, then Jane would have been buried next to her sister and mother in the graveyard of St Nicholas Church in Chawton. When we visited the birds were singing and the primroses were out. Their markers, for feet and head, are plain, with only their names and the dates of death. Jane's mother lived even longer than Cassandra, until she was eighty-seven. It was easy to find their graves, for the grass had

been worn down by the many pilgrims who visit, having been
to Chawton House, now a museum, where the three women
had lived together and where Jane wrote on a little wooden
table, which is still there, in the window. Inside the church
are memorials to the family. This churchyard is not as grand
as Winchester Cathedral, where the spirit really does soar,
but this is a quiet and peaceful corner of England that is, of
course, right out of Austen.

# SIR ARTHUR IGNATIUS CONAN DOYLE

## WRITER AND SPIRITUALIST
### 22 May 1859–7 July 1930
*All Saints Church, Minstead, Hampshire SO43 7EX*

This is the Case of the Mysterious Burial. How did an avowed, not to say evangelical, spiritualist such as Sir Arthur Conan Doyle end up in the graveyard of the ancient All Saints Church in Minstead? It is the loveliest of locations, in a tiny village in the New Forest, his gravestone a Celtic Cross, overlooked only by a straggle of ponies in the adjoining field, beyond which are only trees. On the ledge of his gravestone we found a pipe. I could almost see the smoke curling out of the bowl. The grave is on the southern edge of the graveyard, beneath a spreading oak tree. Visitors, for whom a bench is provided, have left little stones. His epitaph invokes the words of Robert Louis Stevenson: 'Steel true / Blade straight / Arthur Conan Doyle / Knight / Patriot, Physician and man of letters'. His wife Jean is also here; they are 'reunited' in death, as the stone says.

But how did he get here? A cursory investigation of the church reveals that he was buried in 1955, although he died some twenty-five years earlier. Where is Sherlock Holmes when you need him? Not here, I'm afraid, for Sir Arthur killed him off twice and in later years, according to his obituaries, expressed a wish that he should be remembered for his psychic work rather than his novels. On his 71st birthday, he confessed to being tired of hearing about Sherlock. 'Sherlock is dead,' he said. 'I have done with him.' But surely Sir Arthur of all people should know that to be dead is not to be gone.

So back to the case. Here are the facts. Sir Arthur died in his garden at his Crowborough home, Windlesham, in East Sussex at 8.17 a.m. on 7 July 1930, clutching his heart with one hand and a flower in another. His last words, 'You are wonderful,' were to his wife Jean. A few days later he was buried, upright, next to the garden hut that he used as a writing room. Some 200 people attended the funeral. Lady Conan Doyle lived at Windlesham until her death on 27 June 1940 and was buried, also vertically, next to Sir Arthur. In 1955, the family sold the estate.

So where to put the bodies now? According to a bulletin on the Minstead village shop website (our search for clues knows no limits), in 1925 Lady Conan Doyle had purchased a country retreat in Bignell Wood in the New Forest as a 'love gift'. The couple spent a great deal of time here, welcoming visiting mediums and holding séances. Indeed, when alive, Sir Arthur claimed to have had conversations with the spirits of many great men, including Cecil Rhodes, Earl Haig, Joseph Conrad and others. And just after his death, his son Adrian told the press that the family believed Sir Arthur would keep in touch. 'I know perfectly well I am going to have conversations with my father,' he said.

A guide produced for All Saints Church says that Lady Conan Doyle wanted both of them to be buried at Minstead in the first place. It's a beautiful churchyard with a long memory, the earliest graves being from the 1600s. Here too, famously, is the grave of a Mr White whose gravestone includes a cut-out gap before the word 'husband'. It once said 'faithful' before the village gossip reached Mrs White's ears. Anyway, back to 1955. The Church of England, embarrassed by the interest in spiritualism but ever prepared to compromise (as the church guide says!) agreed to the reburial on the condition that the grave was as far away from the church as possible.

Some say that their coffins in Windlesham were dug up in the middle of the night and 'bunged' in a lorry to go to Minstead. Anyway, by whatever means, early one morning in

1955, a lead casket for two containing their remains arrived at the churchyard. The double grave, which had been dug the day before near the far southern boundary, was ready. It was horizontal. There was a short ceremony and the announcement was made. The church guide's source for this was the gravedigger's son, who was helping his father until 10 p.m. the night before, and was a regular at the church. But the story doesn't quite end here. The oak tree, whose branches form an almost claustrophobic canopy over the grave, has been struck by lightning twice, the last time in 1969. What does it mean? We can only all await enlightenment. And how did the pipe get there? The case remains unsolved.

# THOMAS HARDY

## WRITER
### 2 June 1840–11 January 1928
*Ashes: Westminster Abbey, 20 Dean's Yard, London SW1P 3PA*
*Heart: St Michael's Church, Stinsford, Dorset DT2 9QP*

'I do not, in truth, feel much interest in popular opinion of me,' Thomas Hardy told his literary executor, 'and shall sleep quite calmly at Stinsford, whatever happens.'

Well, 'whatever' did indeed happen to Thomas Hardy. The man who was seen as the greatest writer of his time had wanted to be buried at St Michael's Church in Stinsford, the mythical 'Mellstock' of his works and the place where he was baptised, grew up and returned to always for inspiration and solace. He had discussed his wishes with the vicar. But when he died, on 11 January 1928, at the age of eighty-seven, others, including his executor Sydney Cockerell and J. M. Barrie, of *Peter Pan* fame, decided he must instead be buried in Westminster Abbey, as close to Dickens as possible. The nation, along with the great and the good, demanded it. Hardy's family were outraged. Finally the Stinsford vicar came up with a classic English fudge. The body, once cremated, would be buried in the abbey. But his heart would be buried in Stinsford.

Thus, on 16 January, there were two funerals. The first was at Westminster Abbey where Hardy's pallbearers were J. M. Barrie, George Bernard Shaw, John Galsworthy, Rudyard Kipling, A. E. Houseman, Stanley Baldwin and Ramsay MacDonald. Grand, imposing, monumental, if a little bleak weather-wise, with the drizzle outside matching what some thought a feeling of emptiness inside. At the same time, in Stinsford, there was a much simpler service, after which Hardy's heart was taken in a small heart-sized box to be buried in his first wife's grave. It really was most bizarre.

In the pubs, there were jokes about a possible resurrection (Where's the rest of him?) and speculation that a cat ate the heart on the slab.

You cannot visit St Michael's and not feel that, no matter where Hardy's ashes are, he is here in this old graveyard, buried with both his wives, next to parents and grandparents, aunts and uncles, cousins and friends. Hardy fans will find many familiars here, from his poems and novels, under the old yews. For without the likes of Stinsford Church, there would be no Mellstock, no Wessex, and no Tess either. Inside, there is a booklet for sale about Hardy and the church, which traces the many links, both literary and real. This is what it says about Hardy and the grave of his grandfather, also a Thomas, who died in 1837:

'I can tell you to a foot where he's a lying in Mellstock Churchyard at this very moment,' says Dairyman Crick in *Tess*, ' – just between the second yew tree and the north aisle.' On Christmas Eve 1919, Hardy said that he visited the grave to place a sprig of holly on it and claimed to have seen his grandfather's ghost who said, 'A green Christmas,' and walked off into the church.

The air smells fresh and, despite the fact that it is not far from the busy road to Dorchester, rural. The church itself feels intimate. I loved seeing the name 'Angel' on a monument to the Grey family. So that's where he got that one, I thought. It seems that everywhere you look, there is a bit of Thomas Hardy. He sketched the church often (he trained as an architect) and it featured in his poems and novels. There is a stained glass window, based on his favourite Old Testament reading of Elijah and the still small voice (1 Kings 19).

But there is an oddity: at the end of the line of Hardy graves, there is a stone that fairly shouts the name of Cecil Day-Lewis, poet laureate when he died in 1972 and the father of Daniel, the great actor. Cecil is here solely to be near Hardy (or in this case, his heart). It must be the ultimate accolade, the desire to be buried near a figure of inspiration. You see it also in those who crowd round Marx's grave in Highgate. But it does feel rather strange out here, in the heart of Mellstock, to suddenly see someone who was not from that world but who was, essentially, a fan. His stone, grey and rounded, stands proud with this epitaph:

SHALL I BE GONE LONG?

FOR EVER AND A DAY

TO WHOM THERE BELONG?

ASK THE STONE TO SAY

ASK MY SONG

And then, behind, is the grave of his second wife, the actress Jill Balcon, who died in 2009. Her epitaph is equally lovely:

SAYS THE HEART TO THE MIND,

'BELIEVE ME'

SAID THE SHADOW TO THE SUN

'DON'T LEAVE ME'.

I loved this graveyard but it is hard not to see the ironies. Hardy did not want to be in the abbey, but his friends thought he deserved to be next to Dickens, who of course claimed he didn't want to be there either. And then there is Cecil Day-Lewis, whom it is said was refused a plaque in the abbey but was given a plot here in Wessex which, actually, is better anyway.

# FLORENCE NIGHTINGALE

## 12 May 1820–13 August 1910
*St Margaret of Antioch, East Wellow, Hampshire SO51 6DR*

## ATHENA

### OWLET
### 5 June 1850–1855
*Florence Nightingale Museum, St Thomas' Hospital,*
*Westminster Bridge Road, London SE1 7EH*

'Poor little beastie, it was odd how much I loved you,' said Florence Nightingale, shedding a tear over the body of Athena, the owl she had rescued five years before when, as a tiny ball of fluff, it had fallen from its nest in the Parthenon. Florence had been visiting Athens with her older sister, Parthenope, when they came upon children tormenting the tiny owl. 'She was rescued for the sum of six lepta or one farthing. On what slight accidents does fame depend!' wrote Parthenope in her eccentric little 'biography' of Athena, called *Parthenope's Owl Book*.

It is a strange pairing – this little owl and the founder of modern nursing – and yet it is quite fitting and not just because of her avian surname. Florence Nightingale is the lady with the lamp, portrayed as little short of a saint in the way that she brought order out of the chaos of military hospitals in the Crimea. And yet, to achieve that, in that era, as a woman from a well-heeled family, meant that Florence must also have possessed a ruthless stubborn streak coupled with a maverick spirit and an extraordinary will. This is a woman who despaired of the 'gilded cage' occupied by women at the time and insisted to her incredulous family that God was calling her to be a nurse, a job at that time occupied by the working classes and, or so it was claimed, drunken ones at that.

They said no but she refused to budge. She wore her parents down, studying nursing in secret, making herself sick with nerves, turning down several (good) offers of marriage. When she found Athena, her stand-off with her family was at its peak, and what an eccentric pairing they were. The little owl travelled everywhere with Florence, carried in her pocket or a little bag. She fed it meat from her finger daily. 'When set at liberty,' writes Parthenope of the owl, 'she began while sitting on the table, to curtsey and bow with the greatest urbanity'.

I think that the word for *Parthenope's Owl Book* might be 'charming'– exhaustively so. It paints a picture of a rather enclosed, not to say eccentric, literary life. The owl read widely apparently, particularly books about Greece (and in Greek). On her birthday, there was a little party with 'epigrams in her honour' placed in her cage. She would bite and peck strangers, and required a daily 'sand bath'. When Florence's parents finally gave in and allowed Florence to study nursing at Kaiserswerth, a religious community near Dusseldorf, Parthenope took over care for Athena for three months. In 1953 Florence, reunited with Athena, took up a nursing post at a home for gentlewomen in Upper Harley Street, and in 1854, when a cholera epidemic broke out, she rushed to nurse victims in local hospitals. I can only imagine how horrified her genteel family must have been.

This is how Parthenope recorded the events of that summer in Athena's biography:

> Her Mistress had been home after an exceedingly hard summer's work in London with the Cholera added to her usual labours. She had been exceedingly unwell during that too short visit, and had been confined to her bed and her room, for the chief part of it. Athena was her constant companion, when she could bear no one else of larger size, Athena was welcome; she [Athena] sat on the bed and talked to her, she ran races all round the room after imaginary mice. Every meal she considered to have been brought for her especial use and she accordingly appropriated the bread and butter, or pounced upon the chicken, 'Mademoiselle la gâte' was the warning voice, but her Mistress let it be.

When Florence returned to London that autumn, she read in *The Times* of the disaster facing the British Army in the Crimea, with the wounded arriving by the boatload at the British military hospital at Scutari in Constantinople, dying in 'agony' and 'unheeded'. Florence, who was well connected, offered her services and Sidney Herbert, the Secretary of State for War, asked her to lead a group of women nurses to Scutari. Parthenope referred to this trip as Florence's 'great expedition' – and it was during this flurry of activity, when everyone went to London to help, that Athena was left in the attic where, I suppose, it was thought there would be plenty of mice for her to catch. But the owl did not, or could not, hunt. 'The grief and the cold and the isolation were too much for her,' writes Parthenope, 'and when found she was lying dead on her little side, on the very day that her Mistress was to have left England.' She records that the expedition was delayed by a few days and Athena's body was sent to London for embalming. 'Her Mistress asked to see her again, shedding the only tears that she would through that week.'

Thus endeth Athena's story; this, however is where Florence's really begins, for in Scutari, she undertook a crash course in nursing, management and diplomacy. The two hospitals in Scutari were vast, dark and stinking places. In the museum dedicated to her at St Thomas' Hospital in London – where, by the way, Athena perches, head cocked in perpetuity – you get a feeling for how Florence Nightingale used her incredible will to change the way things worked. So not only was she nursing and supervising nurses, changing wounds of badly injured and frostbitten soldiers, she was also writing to their relatives, sending money to widows and organising reading rooms for them and a café where they could buy non-alcoholic drinks. She set up a banking system, allowing solders to send their pay home. Ordinary soldiers adored her and her fame spread: she became the 'lady with the lamp', her image reproduced in pottery figurines, on souvenirs and even paper bags. She hated what she called the 'buzz fuzz' of celebrity but also knew it came with power and influence.

She returned to Britain in 1856, travelling under the name of 'Miss Smith' to avoid publicity. She devoted the rest of her life – which, as she had caught Crimean fever while in Turkey, no one thought would be too long – to improving nursing. In the end, she lived to the incredible age of ninety, by which time she had written some 200 books and begun the Nightingale School at St Thomas', among many other campaigns and ventures. Athena was with her, stuffed of course, until she died. The woman, now a living legend, and the most important woman of her age other than Queen Victoria, still hating the 'buzz fuzz', refused to be buried in

Westminster Abbey. She requested instead to be put in the family plot at East Wellow, near her family home of Embley Park in Hampshire, and that there be just two people accompanying her body to its grave.

St Margaret of Antioch is a very special church. It lies at the end of a road that seems to go on forever, surrounded by farmland. It is not easy to get to today, much less so in 1910 and maybe that was also part of Florence's plan. For her memorial service at St Paul's 3,000 tickets were issued. It was attended by the King and Queen, the Prime Minister, hundreds of nurses and of course the veterans from the Chelsea Hospital who fought in Crimea. Her funeral, though, was a very different affair: her coffin, draped in the white shawl that she wore so often, and bedecked with flowers, was carried on a special funeral train from Waterloo to the tiny station of Romsey in Hampshire. At the foot of the coffin was a cross of mauve orchids fringed with white roses and lilies. Attached was a card signed 'Alexandra' paying tribute to her 'heroism'. It was an ordinary burial service, interspersed with favourite hymns. Her coffin was carried to its grave by six of her 'children', men from the British Army. Seated in the church porch was a bemedalled Crimean veteran, aged eight-two, who had spent three months in Scutari and recalled Florence Nightingale's midnight rounds.

It drizzled that day, which, I think, was perfect. The Nightingale vault, a white pillar stone, stands out in this country churchyard. She has no epitaph, only her initials (again by her request), F. N. She didn't get her wish in that many more than two people went with her to her grave but you can't control everything, even if you are F. N. The day we visited, the church porch was ringed with roses from a wedding the weekend before. This is a Grade I listed building and, inside, we were amazed to see fragments of wall paintings, thought to date from the mid-1200s. There are little tributes to F. N. everywhere, on the windowsill, at the back. Every year in May, on the Sunday nearest her birthday, there is a Nightingale service. When you see this place, and breathe in the air, you know she made the right decision to be buried here, among the ordinary, where she always wanted to be.

# MARY WOLLSTONECRAFT SHELLEY

## WRITER
### 30 August 1797–1 February 1851
*St Peter's Churchyard, Bournemouth, Dorset BH1 2EE*

# MARY WOLLSTONECRAFT GODWIN

## FEMINIST AND WRITER
### 27 April 1759–10 September 1797
*Originally Old St Pancras Churchyard in London,*
*reburied in 1851, St Peter's Churchyard, as above*

It is a dull, dark grey stone placed in a prominent position on the hillside next to the imposing St Peter's Church in Bournemouth. Nothing about it seems dramatic or, indeed, particularly interesting. And yet, underneath lies the human equivalent of a thunderstorm.

This is the (second) grave of pioneer feminist Mary Wollstonecraft and her husband (though, of course, they claimed not to believe in marriage) the radical philosopher William Godwin. Lying between them is their only child, Mary Wollstonecraft Shelley, as she styled herself, the author of the instantly wildly successful *Frankenstein* (published in 1818). She did not know her mother, who died just days after her birth, and was, over her lifetime, often estranged from her father. And yet her wish was to be buried between them. But, for this to happen, they had to be moved to Bournemouth from their (first) grave in Old St Pancras Churchyard in London, which was deemed to be 'dreadful' by Mary Shelley's only surviving child Percy Florence.

Then there is the curious incident of the heart. For the heart of Percy Bysshe Shelley, her husband and one of the original bad boys, is also buried here. It is a fact, though an astounding one, that the 16-year-old Mary and 22-year-old Percy fell in love during their daily walks in Old St Pancras Churchyard. And it was over the (first) grave of her mother that they first declared their love to each other. The only problem – Percy Shelley was already married. They eloped and, after his first wife eventually committed suicide, were married.

Mary Wollstonecraft and William Godwin's story is hardly less chaotic. Indeed, when Mary W. died, he published an admiring memoir but one which, in recounting her affairs and an illegitimate child, hurt her reputation. Thus the great feminist, whose work *A Vindication of the Rights of Woman*, which argued for equal education for girls and boys (hugely radical then), became infamous for her turbulent private life. William Godwin, by the way, did not give their daughter an equal education. Mary met Shelley at her father's house, for the poet was his acolyte and patron. But when they fell in love, William Godwin was aghast.

Confused? If you aren't, you haven't been paying attention. Underneath this grave is a three-generation saga (for Percy Florence is there too): intense, overheated, studded by children, affairs, natural deaths, suicide, poverty, pathos and poetry. Even the story of the heart deserves an Oscar. For Percy Bysshe Shelley drowned in Italy in 1822 and was cremated on a beach, but – according to Byron, and therefore probably not true – his heart refused to burn. His ashes, which were kept in the British consul's wine cellar for a year, were buried beneath his grave in Rome's Protestant cemetery with this epitaph from Shakespeare's *The Tempest*:

> NOTHING OF HIM THAT DOTH FADE
>
> BUT DOTH SUFFER A SEA-CHANGE
>
> INTO SOMETHING RICH AND STRANGE

It is said that, on the first anniversary of Mary Shelley's death, some thirty years after the poet's death, their son opened her box desk. Inside were locks of hair from her three dead children, a notebook that she shared with her husband, a copy of his poem *Adonais* with one page folded round a silk parcel containing the remains of his heart.

So, to sum up: here lie, in addition to Mary Shelley and her son, two people who have another (empty) gravestone in London and one heart that would not burn. It's all a bit much for genteel Bournemouth (which was near to Percy Florence's estate at Boscombe) – the calm after the storm indeed. It certainly makes *Frankenstein* seem almost normal.

*Ian Fleming, St James' Church, Wiltshire*

# THE WEST

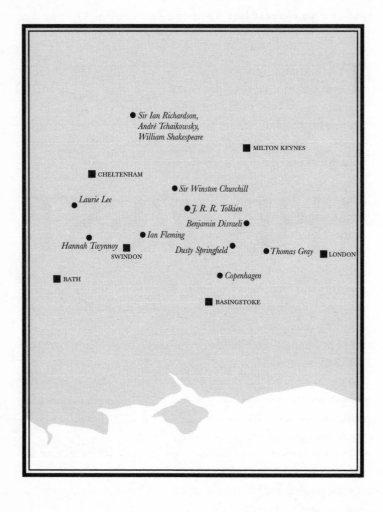

● Sir Ian Richardson,
André Tchaikowsky,
William Shakespeare

■ MILTON KEYNES

■ CHELTENHAM

● Sir Winston Churchill

Laurie Lee ●

● J. R. R. Tolkien

Benjamin Disraeli ●

● Ian Fleming

Hannah Twynnoy ●
SWINDON ■

Dusty Springfield ●

● Thomas Gray  ■ LONDON

■ BATH

● Copenhagen

■ BASINGSTOKE

# SIR WINSTON LEONARD SPENCER CHURCHILL

## POLITICIAN
### 30 November 1874–24 January 1965
*St Martin's Church, Bladon, Oxfordshire OX20 1RS*

The thing that hits you first about Sir Winston Churchill's grave is the size. As a man he was large; as a historical figure, a giant, and surely the man who personified the fight against Hitler. And yet his grave is not grand or particularly imposing: a raised slab, only slightly over-sized, that is shared with his wife Clementine, surrounded by identically sized graves of his family in the quiet churchyard of St Martin's in the village of Bladon in Oxfordshire. He could have been buried in the grounds of nearby Blenheim Palace, his family home. He could have been buried at Westminster Abbey. Or, for that matter, anywhere he wanted.

But he chose Bladon. Anyone can come see him here – and they do. Wear and tear by the constant visitors means the stone has had to be replaced twice. When I came, on a bitterly cold day, there was a small basket of white roses, sent for Clementine. 'On this 1st April, your birthday,' said the card, signed 'Mary'. As a grave, this is one where history looms large, and indeed threatens to overwhelm, but the thing that surprises is this small human touch – a bouquet sent, mostly likely by their daughter, Lady Soames, so many years on (Clementine died in 1977).

He was buried on 30 January 1965. He had lain in state in the ancient stone magnificence of Westminster Hall, endless queues passing by. He had been carried through the streets by gun carriage to a monumental funeral at St Paul's. Big Ben was silenced. The guns at the Tower boomed. Afterwards, the coffin, transferred to a barge, sailed up the Thames and as he passed the London docks, all the cranes dipped towards him, bowing to the old warrior. Then he went by train to Hanborough rail-way station and, finally, by hearse to Bladon.

The church has produced a little booklet about the death and funeral, much of which was gleaned from letters at the time from Mrs Bishop of Beehive Cottage, which adjoins the churchyard, to her sister. Again, it was a joy to find some-thing so personal.

On 24 January, Mrs Bishop wrote:

> We have just heard that the old warrior has given up at last. What a fight he has made! Mr H. from Church Cottage ran over in tears to tell me. He is now tolling the bell – every twenty seconds or so. I expect the same is happening all over England. It is very touching on this lovely morning.

On 30 January, she recounted: 'It is a glorious morning, bitterly cold but no wind and the sun is coming out. I have icicles 8 to 10 inches long in the garden. The village is navy blue! Never have I seen so many police, men and women (900) compressed into such a small place.' People started to queue, she said, in the morning. By the time the (private) funeral was over and they could start to file past, it was four and a half hours from end to graveside. 'The police have put flood lights over the grave so that the queue can carry on after dark ... which they did until midnight.'

On Sunday 31 January: 'The queues restarted at 7 a.m. and continued all day 'til long after dark. The police estimate the numbers at 70,000 during the weekend.'

More than a month later, on 10 February, she adds: 'There is a constant stream of visitors all the time. Lorry and van drivers pull up in the main road and pop up for a moment, business men and travellers, many old folk, school parties and even one or two groups of "mods and rockers" have been in, very quiet and orderly.'

The booklet stops soon after but the visitors who come to see the grave with the word CHURCHILL on the side never have. During the funeral, a poem was read by Richard Dimbleby, his voice breaking. It is included in the booklet and I recount it here for I think it goes some way to explaining why so many of us want to visit him still:

Drop English earth on him beneath
Do our sons, and their sons bequeath his glories
And our pride and grief
At Bladon
For Lionheart that lies below
That feared not toil nor tears nor foe.
Let the oak stand tho tempests blow
At Bladon.
So Churchill sleeps, yet surely wakes
Old Warrior where the morning breaks
On sunlit uplands.
But the heart aches
At Bladon.

## COPENHAGEN

### WAR HORSE
### 1808–12 February 1836
*Stratfield Saye Park and Estate, Stratfield Saye,*
*Hampshire RG7 2BT*

The moment that I turned into the road leading to Stratfield Saye House, I felt, like Alice going down the rabbit hole, that I had gone through a portal into another world. I had come from the swish swish swish of the M4 and the A33 in Hampshire before turning off into an octopus of country roads. And then, finally, I found the gate and once through it I saw, spread in front of me, another England: green on so many levels, tidy tree-lined roads and large quiet fields, grazed by graceful, delicate horses that could have been painted figures on a decorative screen.

There is a calm in the air here and this extraordinary serene atmosphere continued throughout my visit. This carries its own irony, for Stratfield Saye was the home of a warrior, the Duke of Wellington: the Great Duke, military legend and former Prime Minister. But I was not here to see his grave – his colossal monument and tomb are at St Paul's, where military legends must reside – but that of a horse, Copenhagen, his favourite charger, a real life version of Joey, the star of *War Horse*, Michael Morpurgo's story about the First World War. Copenhagen had carried the duke on his back for seventeen hours during the Battle of Waterloo, a fact that stands by itself like a statue to another age.

The house, stables and estate are still owned by the family and open to the public several weeks a year. I came on a sultry day in August and felt as if I had the whole place to myself, though there were a few other visitors. I would never have heard of this place if it wasn't for Copenhagen. But now, walking up the road towards the large house, which is the colour of a burning sun, flanked by the stables, one of which contains the Duke's ludicrously OTT funeral carriage, I was very taken with it, all the more so when I discovered it wasn't even supposed to exist. It seems that after Waterloo in 1815, the nation gave the Great Duke £600,000 to buy a house and estate that would be worthy of such a great national figure. He acquired Stratfield Saye, built in 1630 by Sir William Pitt, as a stop-gap, the plan being to tear it down and build a Blenheim-like palace in its place. Thankfully, for us, the money wasn't there. The whole place, which includes a magical park called 'The Pleasure Grounds', feels intimate.

Copenhagen is buried near the main house, in the middle of a paddock, his gravestone shaded by a huge turkey oak. The Duke bought him when he was five years old and, by all accounts, the stallion did not look like much: chestnut, small, hollow-backed, muscular, compact, with some Arabian blood, and a deserved reputation for being a kicker. 'There may have been many faster horses, no doubt many handsomer, but for bottom and endurance I never saw his fellow,' said Wellington. The horse, who was named after the 1807 battle led by Wellington to capture the Danish Fleet in Copenhagen harbour, carried him through the Peninsular Campaign and, of course, at Waterloo.

It is hard to imagine Copenhagen's equivalent today. He was fêted and painted (there are many portraits of him in the Music Room in the house), his body, in idealised form, the stuff of statues. He retired to Stratfield Saye where he was indulged as a family pet and died on 12 February 1836, aged twenty-eight. He was buried here, with full military honours. (Apparently, a few years later, a museum requested that Copenhagen be disinterred, so his skeleton could be displayed alongside Marengo, Napoleon's horse. The duke refused.)

The duke's son gave Copenhagen a headstone and an

epitaph: 'Here Lies Copenhagen, The Charger ridden by The Duke of Wellington, the entire day at the battle of Waterloo. Born 1808, Died 1836. *God's humbler instrument, though meaner clay / Should share the glory of that glorious day.*' After visiting the grave, I took a walk along the garden path, perfumed with lavender, flitted over by painted lady butterflies, before heading over to the Pleasure Grounds. This place is of another world, another time, when war horses were real.

# BENJAMIN DISRAELI, EARL OF BEACONSFIELD

## POLITICIAN
### 21 December 1804–19 April 1881
*St Michael and All Angels Church, Hughenden Valley, High
Wycombe, Bucks HP14 4LA*

Benjamin Disraeli, probably the greatest Conservative
Prime Minister ever, did not want a state funeral. The
news was revealed in his will: 'I desire and direct that I may
be buried in the same vault in the churchyard of Hughenden
in which the remains of my late dear wife Mary Ann Disraeli
were placed and that my funeral may be conducted with the
same simplicity as hers.' When William Gladstone heard
what his great political foe had decided, he harrumphed: 'In
death he remains as he was in life: all show and no substance.'
But, actually, I would have thought the opposite.

Certainly when you drive up the hill the 'Church in
the Park' – as St Michael and All Angels, set among fields
in the Hughenden Valley, has always been called – is hardly in
the same realm as Westminster Abbey. If you continue up the
hill, you will find Hughenden Manor, the house that Disraeli
nearly bankrupted himself to buy in 1848. Dizzy, as he was
called, was intent on climbing 'the greasy pole' (a phrase
he invented), despite his many drawbacks. The archetypal
outsider, he was born Jewish and, though not poor, certainly
wasn't rich or aristocratic. But he was a charmer, a great flirt,
a talented writer and politician, smart and (hugely) ambitious. Disraeli said he owed all his success in life to the women
he knew and so it is perfect that he was buried between two
of them. Inside the church, there is a tribute from a third,
Queen Victoria, for he was a favourite of hers.

The family vault is outside, abutting the church, headed
with Victorian arches, surrounded by some rather garish blue

railings. To Disraeli's left is his wife Mary Anne. When they married she was a 47-year-old wealthy widow, he an ambitious 35-year-old. 'Dizzy married me for my money,' she once said, 'but if he had a chance to do it again, he would marry me for love.' After their wedding, she paid off his debts and purchased a grand home for them in London, but Disraeli also desperately wanted a country seat. He borrowed heavily to buy Hughenden and all of Mary Anne's shrewd budgeting couldn't compensate for it. In the end, it was only through the largesse of another woman that they were able to keep it.

When you visit the grave, it is quite confusing to see among all the Disraelis the name of Sarah Brydges Willyams, from Cornwall. She is to the right of him, a place that she secured out of sheer bribery. It turns out that Mrs Brydges Willyams was a fan of Disraeli's politics and novels. She wrote to him to say so and he wrote back. Like him, she was a Christian of Jewish parents, but unlike him she was wealthy. The Disraelis became friends with her, paying annual visits. Mrs Brydges Willyams said she would make him her heir, but in return she wanted to be buried next to him in the family plot. So this is how she got there. The £30,000 that she left him in her will allowed him to pay off the mortgage.

The funeral was recorded fully by *The Times* on 27 April 1881. 'On a green hillside there were collected a greater number, perhaps, of illustrious and well-known personages than ever assembled in one place in the open air so far away from the capital,' it reported. 'The first impressive and unmistaken feature of the gathering was the unaffected regret, the sincere and evidently unexaggerated feeling of sorrow.' Mr Gladstone was unable to attend (much, I suspect, to Mr Disraeli's pleasure). The Queen, who was represented by the Prince of Wales, sent a wreath of wild primroses from her home in the Isle of Wight. On a card affixed to the flowers, she wrote: 'His favourite flowers; from Osborne, a tribute of affection and regret from Queen Victoria.'

Benjamin Disraeli had a talent for friendship, even with someone as elevated as the Queen. When he was Prime Minister, he wrote to her daily with entertaining flair. After her husband's death, he was a consolation and helped bring her back into the public sphere. Disraeli certainly was not above a bit of unctuousness: 'You have heard me called a flatterer and it is true. Everyone likes flattery; and when you come to royalty, you should lay it on with a trowel.' And now, after his death, she repaid his efforts, making her own pilgrimage to Hughenden a few days after his funeral. She walked the route of his cortège and gave a memorial to the church which hangs above his pew seat today. It says:

TO THE DEAR AND HONOURED MEMORY OF
BENJAMIN, EARL OF BEACONSFIELD.

THIS MEMORIAL IS PLACED BY HIS GRATEFUL
SOVEREIGN AND FRIEND VICTORIA R.I.

'KINGS LOVETH HIM THAT SPEAKETH RIGHT'

And not loveth just by kings – but queens too. Later, in the dining room at Hughenden Manor, now run by the National Trust, I could see again how all of the women in his life came together. Looking down on us was a huge portrait of Victoria, whom he called The Faery, dominating what he liked to call his 'Gallery of Affection'. It is also here that his wife would preside over their frequent dinner parties for which Mrs Brydges Willyams, who seems quite omnipresent, often would send gifts of food, such as lobster.

## IAN LANCASTER FLEMING

### WRITER
### 28 May 1908–12 August 1964
*St James' Church, Sevenhampton, Wiltshire SN6 7QA*

You approach Ian Fleming's grave on foot, via a path that leads to the austere St James' Church, which is set back from the road that meanders through the well-tended village of Sevenhampton in Wiltshire. I see his grave immediately: a tall, graceful obelisk, set against the impressively large stone church. Behind the churchyard is an intensely green field that is filled with what seems a huge number of brown cows. I may have seen too many Bond films but I immediately imagined 007 arriving by helicopter in that field, cows scattering in all directions, bellowing and mooing, as he walks over to join the mourners at his creator's funeral.

We love Bond. I am not sure we love Ian Fleming quite as much but then, of course, he had the handicap of being real. It's interesting that he chose to be buried here in the middle of an English idyll (although one that, these days, is alarmingly close to Swindon and its many roundabouts). Although he was a one-off, by definition, he was also an English type: Eton, academic failure, Sandhurst, naval intelligence during the Second World War, journalism, writer, womaniser, drinker, larger than life (and, just to show another side, bibliophile).

It soon becomes apparent that this is not one grave but three, the obelisk holding a trio of oval slate plaques, all with graceful, subdued, calligraphy. His epitaph says: 'Omnia perfunctus vitae praemia marces'. If you are being prim, you can translate this as 'Having enjoyed all life's prizes, now you decay'. Or, of course, there's 'You are rotting away now having had a good life'. His glamorous wife, Ann, with whom he had a fierce and tempestuous relationship, is the next name I see as I circle, ever observant of the cows. She died in 1981. Her epitaph reads: 'There is no one like her, no one'. And then around the next side there is a third slate, to their only son, Caspar, who died in 1975, having committed suicide. On his slate is a quote from Keats: 'to cease upon the midnight with no pain'. Here lies, then, the whole family.

Why Sevenhampton? They had a rather grand house near there and, to be honest, I think it's perfect, but I suppose in many ways it really should be Jamaica, where they had a place that Fleming called Goldeneye, named after the code-word for a naval intelligence operation he had masterminded during the war. This is where he wrote his novels, but only after he married Ann, with whom he'd been having an affair while she had been married to Viscount Rothermere, owner of the *Daily Mail*. Obviously Fleming wrote – he was a journalist – but she had been urging him to write fiction, and in 1952 he took her up on it. 'I was in the process of getting married,' he said, 'which is a very painful thing to do at the age of forty-four, so to take my mind off the whole business, I sat down and wrote a novel.'

That was *Casino Royale*. Thus we met Bond (007, licensed to kill) and a plot that would become familiar: gambling, a martini (shaken not stirred), luxury, ruthlessness and, of course, beautiful women. The world, though not the literary one, loved it, but it was the fact that President Kennedy had it on his bedside table that clinched the deal (a very Bond-like detail, I think). Fleming, who was accused of trading in sex and sadism, had this to say:

I wanted to show a hero without any characteristics, who was simply the blunt instrument in the hands of the government, then he started eating a number of meals and dressing in a certain way so that he became encrusted with characteristics much against my will. Apart from the fact that he wears the same clothes that I wear, he and I really have very little in common. I do rather envy him his blondes and his efficiency, but I can't say I much like the chap.

By the time he died, from his second heart attack, at the age of fifty-six, books about that 'chap' had sold twenty million. He had left his day job on newspapers to write novels full time in 1959. There was, as *The Times* notes in his rather subdued obituary, a 'snowball of success'. Each book was a bestseller. Bond was imitated and parodied and then, of course, came the films and Sean Connery. But, despite all of this, Fleming's private life was a mess. He had many affairs and his wife had a 'passionate friendship', as the *Daily Mail* put it when serialising her memoir, with Labour leader Hugh Gaitskell. Fleming had also been drinking a bottle of gin and smoking seventy cigarettes a day, and in 1961 he had had his first heart attack.

He did end up in the place that, I think, is perfect for him. Looking at the cows, I see the location shot of the ancient, beautiful English church and the row of trees on the other side leading off to who knows where. There are many theories as to who Bond was. There is Fleming's war-time friend Patrick Dalzel-Job – whose grave is covered in this book – and others too, not to mention Fleming himself. But a more prosaic answer is that he was the author of a book called Macmillan's *Field Guide to Birds of the West Indies* and it was his name, on the book cover as it lay on a table at Goldeneye, that Ian Fleming saw when he decided the time had come to write something down.

# THOMAS GRAY

## POET
### 26 December 1716–30 July 1771
*St Giles Church, Church Lane, Stoke Poges,*
*Buckinghamshire SL2 4NZ*

My first mistake was thinking that Stoke Poges Parish Church was, in fact, in the village of Stoke Poges. I drove around in circles for some time before stopping at a random house.

'You're nowhere near,' said the villager. 'St Giles was the patron saint of beggars and so it's outside the village.'

I headed off down the road towards, whisper it, Slough. And when I found St Giles, it was indeed perilously close to the dreaded place, not so much part of the village as an island of picturesque-ness in the upmarket suburbia that serves as the buffer between Stoke Poges and Slough. The church and graveyard may be in Buckinghamshire but only just.

My second mistake was thinking that Thomas Gray, author of *Elegy Written in a Country Graveyard*, thought to have been written in St Giles and where he is buried, would have his own grave. I searched for some time, honing in on the oldest part of the graveyard around the church, part of which is Saxon. The headstones were intriguing, not least because some of them would have been there at the time Gray wrote his great poem:

> Beneath those rugged elms, that yew-tree's shade,
>   Where heaves the turf in many a mould'ring heap,
> Each in his narrow cell for ever laid,
>   The rude Forefathers of the hamlet sleep.

The rugged elms are gone but the yews remain, shading the gravestones of the forefathers of Gray's masterful reflection on poverty, ambition and remembrance. But where was Thomas Gray's narrow cell? I asked in the church and was directed not towards the ground but to a plaque fixed to the church wall.

OPPOSITE TO THIS STONE, IN THE SAME TOMB UPON WHICH
HE HAS SO FEELINGLY RECORDED HIS GRIEF AT THE LOSS OF A
BELOVED PARENT ARE DEPOSITED THE REMAINS OF
THOMAS GRAY ... BURIED AUGUST 6 1771.

I examine the tomb, which is of red brick with a weathered slab top. The inscription says that the vault holds Mary Antrobus, who died unmarried 5 November 1749, aged sixty-six.

IN THE SAME PIOUS CONFIDENCE, BESIDE HER FRIEND AND SISTER,
HERE SLEEP THE REMAINS OF DOROTHY GRAY, WIDOW,
THE CAREFUL, TENDER MOTHER OF MANY CHILDREN, ONE OF
WHOM ALONE HAD THE MISFORTUNE TO SURVIVE HER. SHE DIED
MARCH 11, 1753, AGED 57.

So Thomas Gray was buried with his mother, who was buried with her sister, the husband and his father nowhere near. After a little research, it did not seem so odd for behind that epitaph lies a tale about Dorothy: of an awful marriage to a wife-beater, of giving birth to twelve children, all of whom but Thomas died in infancy, of a milliner who refused to leave her shop in London in order to help support her son. Her brother was an assistant master at Eton, where she sent Thomas when he was only eight, to escape his father. There he thrived, shy, serious, reserved, sowing the seed for a life of intellectual and literary pursuits.

The rest is history, not to mention poetry. *The Elegy* is one of the best loved and most recited poems in the English language. It is often cited by politicians as a favourite, its themes of poverty, class, remembrance still relevant today:

> The boast of heraldry, the pomp of pow'r,
>   And all that beauty, all that wealth e'er gave,
> Await alike th' inevitable hour:
>   The paths of glory lead but to the grave.

As I headed out of the churchyard, there was one further surprise, for the man who wrote so movingly about the graves of others but did not wish for one himself is remembered in the adjoining meadow, which is known as Gray's Field, and is now owned by the National Trust. It felt marvellously random to walk out of the churchyard, go through a gate into that newly mown meadow and find, to one side, a whacking great monument surrounded by a riot of wild-flowers. God knows what Thomas Gray would have made of this giant stone pedestal topped by a stone sarcophagus, its panels inscribed with verses from his *Elegy*. But, as it was erected in 1799, he never saw it, which, is probably just as well.

# LAURENCE EDWARD ALAN 'LAURIE' LEE

## WRITER
### 26 June 1914–13 May 1997
*Holy Trinity Church, Slad Road, Slad, Gloucestershire GL6 7QA*

Laurie Lee's grave is in the perfect position, just to the left, near the top of the steep path that leads up from the busy, winding Slad Road to Holy Trinity Church. 'He lies in the valley he loved,' says the stone, the top of which is embellished with a scattering of (stone) wild-flowers. On the other side is the opening verse from his poem, *April Rise*. When he was dying, in that month, his daughter Jessie tells how she asked him to pick a poem to read and that is the one that he chose. This is the beginning:

> If ever I saw blessing in the air
>  I see it now in this still early day
> Where lemon-green the vaporous morning drips
>  Wet sunlight on the powder of my eye.

We stood, looking beyond the stone, to the valley that he loved. It is the perfect English view, trees, fields, hedgerows; I think it should be listed. If you can list the Beatles' Abbey Road pedestrian crossing, then I don't see why you can't list a view – this view, the perfect accompaniment to Laurie Lee's words. Plus, a 'Grade II listed view' would put paid to the endless attempts by house-builders to 'develop' this place. This bit of Gloucestershire is crowded enough already. Surely this valley could do without more concrete. The village of Slad lies between places called Paradise and Purgatory Wood and that too feels appropriate. The road there is hellishly busy, the traffic going too fast. But then, after some perilous parking, we were up in the graveyard, looking at the view, organ music wafting over us.

We went inside, the organists oblivious to us, and found the stained glass window dedicated to Lee. I have seen quite a few memorial windows and this is one of the best: the stained glass crisp and clean, the country scenes so fresh that you could smell the grass. Some parts of the window have been left clear and, through it, you can see the trees outside. On the window is this quote from *Cider with Rosie*:

> I remember, too, the light on the slopes, long shadows in tufts and hollows, with cattle, brilliant as painted china, treading their echoing shapes. Bees blew like cake-crumbs through the golden air, white butterflies like sugared wafers, and when it wasn't raining a diamond dust took over which veiled and yet magnified all things.

When you are finished at the church, you can just go down, cross the road, and have a cider, if not with Rosie, then surely for Laurie Lee, at his local, The Woolpack. And, as long as we are embarking on this mission, the pub could be listed as well as the view, so that everyone can see his world.

## SIR IAN WILLIAM RICHARDSON

### ACTOR
**7 April 1934–9 February 2007**
*Underneath the Royal Shakespeare Theatre, Waterside,*
*Stratford-upon-Avon, Warwickshire CV37 6BB*

## ANDRÉ TCHAIKOWSKY (BORN ROBERT ANDRZEJ KRAUTHAMMER)

### MUSICIAN AND SKULL
**1 November 1935–26 June 1982**
*Royal Shakespeare Company props cupboard, Stratford-upon-Avon*

The scene: Centre stage, Royal Shakespeare Theatre, Stratford, April 2013. It is *Hamlet*, Act 5, Scene 1, in the graveyard.

Hamlet: 'Alas, poor Yorick!' [holding the skull aloft] 'I knew him, Horatio, a fellow of infinite jest, of most excellent fancy.'

Sitting in the audience, I peered at the skull. I glanced down at the front of the stage where a woman in a red dress was sitting, staring up at the skull. She may not have known it but she could have been right between two ghosts. For below her, or at least somewhere in the front row, in the concrete foundations of the theatre, finished in 2010, lay the ashes of the great actor Sir Ian Richardson. And in front of her was a skull which could have once been attached to André Tchaikowsky, a pianist and Shakespeare fan who willed it to the RSC after he died in 1982.

Isn't all of this just a little spooky?

I imagined Sir Ian's long, thin face, his aquiline nose twitching faintly. 'You might think that,' he would say, 'I couldn't possibly comment.' And then he'd arch an eyebrow at us. That was his catchphrase. Sir Ian may have been a great Shakespearean actor but it is for his role as the scheming politician Francis Urquhart in the TV hit *House of Cards* (the 1990 series) that he will be remembered by many.

Of course, if anyone knew about political skulduggery, it was Francis Urquhart. *House of Cards* and its two sequels were shown against the only slightly less murderous but entirely real background of the overthrow of Margaret Thatcher, the sleaze of the John Major years and the rise and rise of political spin. The age of deference, of believing what politicians said, had come to a juddering halt, with Mr Urquhart – and no doubt Shakespeare too – looking on approvingly.

All theatres like to boast a ghost but few have one as eminent as Sir Ian, who died in 2007 at the age of seventy-two. A year later, his son Miles, also an actor, had taken his mother Maroussia to see the new theatre being built. 'The building was at the foundation stage, the cement mixers were churning and, on impulse, I turned to my mother and said: "Why don't we put Dad's ashes in one of those?"'

His ashes had been on the mantelpiece at home since his death and, as Sir Ian had been a founding member of the RSC, it seemed right. Lasers were used to pinpoint the exact spot in the foundations that would eventually be under the front row. 'My father will be in the front row for every performance,' said Miles, 'and just where he liked to be, centre stage.' There is a small plaque commemorating this, but not over the exact spot.

Looking up, eyebrows arching (obviously), Sir Ian would have had a much better view of the skull than I did. André came to Britain after the Second World War, having escaped Nazi-occupied Warsaw, changing his name in the process. A musical prodigy, he became a composer and concert pianist, living in Oxford, with frequent forays to Stratford-upon-Avon. It was discovered only after his death at forty-six from colon cancer that André had donated his body to science but had requested that his skull be given to the RSC for 'use in theatrical performance'.

The Home Office ruled that this was legal and the RSC accepted the skull but, for many years, André hardly left the prop cupboard. Indeed such was the squeamishness that an exact replica of his skull, complete with gold teeth, was made. As David Howells, curator of the RSC archive, said: 'In 1989 the actor Mark Rylance rehearsed with it for quite a while but he couldn't get past the fact it wasn't Yorick's, it was André Tchaikowsky's. That, and the fear of an accident and it being slightly macabre, was why they decided not to use it and used an exact replica.'

Then, in 2008, *Hamlet* director Greg Doran decided that André's big moment had come. He would be held aloft by David Tennant of *Doctor Who* fame. 'It was sort of a little shock tactic ... though, of course, to some extent that wears off and it's just André, in his box,' Doran said. The production was a huge hit and André went with it to London. Then there was a TV production and, perhaps the ultimate in true immortality, a first class stamp showing David Tennant holding the skull and saying (maybe): 'Alas, poor André, I knew him...'

# WILLIAM SHAKESPEARE

## PLAYWRIGHT AND POET
### 23 April 1564–23 April 1616
*Holy Trinity Church, Old Town, Stratford-upon-Avon CV37 6BG*

Holy Trinity is a handsome and capacious church on the banks of the Avon and, outside, on the path up to the front door, there was this sandwich board sign:

> Holy Trinity Church
> With Shakespeare's
> Grave Inside
> OPEN

I laughed for that really would be news. Doubters, researchers and those who are just plain curious have been trying to get Shakespeare's grave opened more or less since he died in 1616, not to see his body so much as to ascertain if any of his manuscripts are there too.

Obviously it was the church that was open, not the grave but, still, it does not disappoint. Holy Trinity is an ancient and lovely church on the banks of the Avon, an easy walk along the riverbank from the town centre and theatre where, the night before, I had seen *Hamlet*. 'Thou know'st 'tis common; all that lives must die,' says Gertrude to Hamlet, 'passing through nature to eternity'.

Eternity certainly has been Shakespeare's, and an eternal mystery surrounds the man himself. Very little is really known about him and much of what is known comes from this church. This is where he was baptised ('Gulielmus filius Johannes Shakspeare' [William the son of John Shakespeare] it says) on 26 April 1564. By the time he died the records were in English and it says, on 25 April 1616, 'Will Shakspeare,

Gent'. His grave is in the chancel – and he would have had to pay for such a prominent spot. Maybe it is because this church provides such a marvellous setting: from the tiny door you stoop through to enter to the magnificent stained glass to the fifteenth-century misericords, it is a delight. An elderly gentleman sat in the aisle, collecting £2 for those wishing to see the grave. It seemed a small price.

The grave is, of course, mysterious. His wife, Anne Hathaway, whom he famously gave only his 'second best bed' in his will, is next to him. Her epitaph, translated from Latin, begins, 'Breasts, O mother, milk and life thou didst give'. It ends 'Come quickly, Christ, that my mother, though shut within this tomb may rise again and reach the stars.' It is thought this was written on behalf of their daughter Susanna, who is also buried nearby, as is her husband John Hall. But there is no trace of others in the family, including their two other children.

His grave has no name or dates. Surely, of any man who has ever lived, Shakespeare should not want for elegant epitaphs. And yet this is engraved on his slab:

> GOOD FRIEND FOR JESUS SAKE FORBEARE
> TO DIGG THE DUST ENCLOASED HEARE
> BLESTE BE Y MAN Y SPARES THES STONES
> AND CURST BE HE Y MOVES MY BONES.

The slab is overlooked from the wall by a bust of the man himself: chubby, balding, moustachioed and staring straight ahead, quill in hand. It sits in a niche, enriched by cherubs and topped by a skull, though not, as far as we know at least, poor Yorick's. But that's another story…

# DUSTY SPRINGFIELD

## SINGER
### 16 April 1939–2 March 1999
*St Mary the Virgin, Hart Street, Henley-on-Thames, Oxfordshire RG9 2AU*

Dusty Springfield is, by common consent, one of the greatest soul singers of all time; and so you have to ask, what's a girl like that doing in the graveyard of Henley-on-Thames? Well, I think you would have to answer: livening the whole place up a bit. Her gravestone provides a much-needed splash of colour in the unremittingly good taste palette of Henley – the blue of the river, the grey stone bridge, the gorgeous ancient church of St Mary the Virgin. And there, right before you as you walk into the churchyard, hard to avoid, really, is a stone surrounded by eight pots of colour – a dash of geranium red, begonia orange, pink, purple, yellow white, all topped with bunches of fading flowers in crumpled cellophane.

The stone says merely: Dusty Springfield, OBE. 1939 – 1999. It wasn't her real name (Mary Isobel Catherine Bernadette O'Brien, as you ask) but then Dusty, a childhood name for a tomboy, and Springfield, apparently dreamt up in a field one spring in Somerset during a photo shoot for her new group, was the only name that most of us knew her by. Sometimes less is more but that was not really Dusty's style. Dusty was an icon of the sixties: blonde hair, heavy make-up, a troubled soul whose songs provided the soundtrack for so many of our lives. She died, of breast cancer, aged fifty-nine, with hundreds of fans, not to mention the likes of Lulu, attending her funeral in Henley where she lived in her later years. Personally, I would like to have seen a lyric added to that stone, maybe this from one of her big hits, 'I Only Want to Be with You': 'You don't have to stay forever, I will understand…'

# JOHN RONALD REUEL TOLKIEN

## WRITER AND PROFESSOR
### 3 January 1892–2 September 1973
*Wolvercote Cemetery, Banbury Road, Oxford OX2 2EE*

To find J. R. R. Tolkien's grave in the large Wolvercote Cemetery in Oxford, you need to look down and follow the small signs placed on the verges. It makes sense for, surely, the placement makes it easier for diminutive hobbits and other races of Middle Earth who may want – and who can say they don't? – to visit the grave of their creator. Tolkien could have chosen many ways to describe himself on the gravestone. He was a CBE, the Merton Professor of English Language and Literature at Oxford from 1945 until his retirement in 1959, and one of the best writers, as well as one of the best-selling authors, of all time. So what does it say? Simply 'Beren'. And, after his wife Edith's name, it says 'Luthien'. These were their Middle-Earth names. In Middle Earth, Luthien was a beautiful princess who forsook her own immortality for her love of the mortal warrior Beren. It is a hugely romantic tale, as was theirs.

Their combined grave looks a bit as if it has been furnished by magpies, full of shiny bits and other offerings from fans. 'Thanks for everything,' says a bit of paper, rolled up. A small doll is wedged into a mound of ivy. There are candles and a lamp, other tiny messages, ribbons, bunches of flowers and two rosaries draped on a rose bush. The Hungarian Tolkien Society has been here, as have others. *The Silmarillion*, which was published posthumously, is there, the pages opened to the chapter on Luthien and Beren. This is a grave of pilgrimage, for hobbits and humans too.

# HANNAH TWYNNOY

## BARMAID
### 1670 (date unknown)– 23 October 1703
*Malmesbury Abbey Graveyard, Gloucester Street,*
*Malmesbury, Wiltshire SN16 0AA*

# GEORGE WOMBWELL

## MENAGERIST
### 24 December 1777–16 November 1850
*Highgate Cemetery (West), Swains Lane, London N6 6PJ*

# FRANK C. BOSTOCK

## LION-TAMER AND SHOWMAN
### 10 September 1866–8 October 1912
*Abney Park Cemetery, Stoke Newington High Street,*
*London N16 0LH*

'Lions and tigers and bears, oh my!'
Dorothy as she skipped down the Yellow Brick Road in *The Wizard of Oz*

This, then, is my menagerist corner. It is not possible for any of the above to have known each other personally (though Bostock and Wombwell were related) but all of them were obsessed with big cats and all have remarkable graves. But, of the three, Hannah is the odd one out in that she was the first person to be killed by a tiger in Britain while Wombwell and Bostock owned lions and tigers (and bears).

'Oh my!' is the only real reaction to Hannah's gravestone, which lies in the graveyard of the imposing Malmesbury Abbey in calmest Wiltshire. It records that she died on 23 October 1703, aged thirty-three years and adds:

IN BLOOM OF LIFE

SHE SNATCHED FROM HENCE

SHE HAD NOT ROOM

TO MAKE DEFENCE:

FOR TYGER FIERCE

TOOK LIFE AWAY

AND HERE SHE LIES

IN A BED OF CLAY.

UNTIL RESURRECTION DAY

The tale is filled out, slightly, by the discovery of a plaque in Hullavington Church in a nearby village. The memorial no longer exists, of course, for that is often the way with tiger tales. But the plaque, when it did exist, apparently said that Hannah had worked at a pub called the White Lion (roar) when, in 1703, a travelling menagerie set up in the pub's rear garden. Hannah took a shine to the tiger, teasing it, despite remonstrations from its keeper. One day, the tiger somehow escaped from its enclosure and tore her to pieces. Hannah's tombstone may be small, but it has made her famous, at least in Malmesbury, where on the 300th anniversary of her death, all the girls in the town named Hannah put a flower on her grave.

George Wombwell, born near Saffron Walden in Essex, was supposed to be a cordwainer or shoe maker. He'd moved to London in 1804 but life got much more colourful, not to say dangerous, when he bought two boa constrictors at the London docks and started showing them in local pubs (some of which, I imagine, were called the White Lion). This was the beginning of an extraordinary life. By 1810, he was travelling the country with an exceptional menagerie of animals including elephants, giraffes, monkeys, kangaroos, ostriches and, naturally, snakes. It also included six lions, three tigers and, oh my, we must assume bears. Wombwell bred and raised many animals himself though was also remarkably unsentimental. There is a good tale that, during one fair, the Wombwell elephant died and a rival put up a sign boasting 'The Only Live Elephant in the Fair'. George promptly erected a sign proclaiming 'The Only Dead Elephant in the Fair', explaining that to see a dead elephant was truly extraordinary, a sight never to be seen again. Guess who had the longest queue? The menagerie, which would be illegal today, of course, was then also viewed as a sort of travelling natural history museum, though one played in by a brass band.

But it is the lions that roar out at you, not least because, on top of George's tomb, is the most magnificent stone version of one. This is, or was, Nero, his very tame pet lion which apparently let children ride on his back and slept in the same room as George. Another lion, said to be the first lion bred in captivity in Britain, was named Wallace after Scottish rebel William Wallace. Wombwell actually organised lion fights with both of these, the dogs facing Nero surviving in much better shape than those that encountered Wallace who, over the years, killed at least one man but it was deemed that it was the man's fault (oh my!) and it only added to his lore. In the end Wallace, stuffed, was put on display at Saffron Walden museum.

I think Nero got the better deal, reclining magisterially among Highgate's jungle of greenery. Wombwell, when he died, was described this way by *The Times*:

His enterprise and perseverance, coupled with the possession of sound judgement and strict integrity, had gained for the deceased considerable wealth, and he has long maintained the position of being the largest proprietor of wild animals in the world. No one probably has done so much to forward practically the study of natural history amongst the masses, for his menageries visited every fair and every town in the kingdom and were everywhere popular.

George Wombwell had decided that, as he had spent so much time living with his animals, he wanted to die with them as well. Thus, he had a travelling bed-carriage made and it is in this that he duly died, while the menagerie was at Northallerton. *The Times* recorded: 'An announcement of his death was made by his own request to the spectators, after which the band played the "Dead March" in *Saul*, the animals were fed and the exhibition closed for the evening.' Even his coffin has a tiger tale to tell. It seems that Prince Albert had consulted George over why his dogs were dying and Wombwell had ascertained that their water was poisoning them. The prince, to reciprocate the kindness, gave him some oak timber from the recently salvaged HMS *Royal George*. Wombwell fashioned a coffin made for himself and promptly put it on display – for a fee! So this is the coffin he was buried in, under Nero's considerable weight, with an epitaph that said, in parenthesis, Menagerist.

This brings us to our final big cat, the stone lion that lies, sleeping, over Frank C. Bostock's grave in Abney Park in Stoke Newington. The Bostocks originally worked with the Wombwell menagerie but they became family when, in 1852, George Wombwell's niece Emma married a Bostock (though Hannah, sadly, cannot be linked in any way). The result was three sons, all of whom would become showmen. Frank was known as the Great USA Showman, to distinguish him from his brothers.

His obituary, in the *World's Fair* newspaper, recounted that Frank's father, also a showman, of course, had planned for this son to go into the Church. Frank had other ideas. 'His father's lion-tamer got badly mauled after roughly treating a lion, and Frank asked to take his place,' the obituary recalled. 'His father refused but the next day found his young son in the lion's cage. "If you come out of there alive, I'll thrash you," said the elder Bostock but the youngster got through his task with such success that he was allowed to continue.'

Thus, at age fifteen, Frank C. Bostock became a lion-tamer. At twenty-seven, he went to New York. The National Fairground Archive, at the University of Sheffield, records that it is said that he and his family lived in one caravan while two other wagons held four monkeys, five parrots, three lions, a sheep and a boxing kangaroo. He would make a name for himself in the States with his touring menagerie. Frank thought big, creating extravagant themed parks such as Dreamland at Coney Island and, when he returned to England, something called The Jungle, a massive touring exhibit. But always, at the core, were Frank and his lions.

There is a picture of Frank on stage with twenty lions. His training technique revolved around kindness, not cruelty, and he wrote a book, *The Training of Wild Animals*, which has such memorable chapter headings as 'Housekeeping for Wild Animals' and 'The Feeding of Snakes and Elephants'. His obituary gives you a flavour of the man: 'Of magnificent physique, standing well over 6 feet high, with handsome features and a perpetual smile, Frank Bostock made a fine figure in his gala dress for the ring, and for many years gave untold enjoyment to thousands of youngsters and adults by his daring and clever feats with wild animals'. He had 'many' escapes from death over the years, being mauled by lions and tigers. (If only Hannah had known Frank, she might have survived.) There was one particularly colourful anecdote involving one of his lions named Wallace who was, he said, 'notorious'. I think we know who that lion was named after.

He died, aged forty-six, at his home in Kensington from flu. He had more than 1,000 animals in his shows in America, Australia, Europe and South Africa. The report of his funeral, again in the *World's Fair*, sounds like the greatest gathering of showmen on earth, with thirty carriages of mourners, the streets being lined with crowds. And the flowers! Oh my! The White City Jungle, of London, sent a wreath of a tiger's head, the Wild Australia Company sent a kangaroo in flowers, a life-sized lion came from the Manchester Jungle and the Showman of Earl's Court sent a painting of a lion surrounded by roses.

Frank's grave doesn't give much away. I suppose if he had one word on it that would be 'showman'. But then do you really need much when you've got a lion on your grave? My question: is Frank's lion related, in some way, to George's? And what would Hannah say about it all except, of course: 'Oh my!'

*Boatswain (Byron's dog), Newstead Abbey, Nottinghamshire*

# THE MIDLANDS

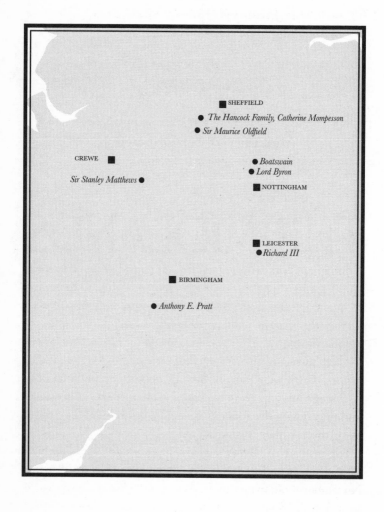

# BARON GEORGE GORDON BYRON

## POET
### 22 January 1788–19 April 1824
*St Mary Magdalene Church, Hucknall, Notts NG15 7AS*

## BOATSWAIN

## PET
### May 1803–18 November 1808
*Newstead Abbey, Nottinghamshire NG15 9HJ*

It's all ended rather badly for Byron, but then, I guess, we shouldn't be surprised about that. Of course, if the great man had his way he would be buried in a spot of high romanticism, in the grounds of Newstead Abbey in Nottinghamshire where, presuming he had access to a periscope (entirely possible in his case), he would have a view of the magnificent ruined chapel and, beyond that, a lake. To the other side, he would overlook The Great Garden where, behind the mirrored rectangular pond, in the middle of the tousled lawn, are two statues, mossy satyrs with bunches of grapes, which were placed there by one of Byron's ancestors. As a scene it is gorgeous: totally English, redolent of romance and tinged with decadence. Surely, I thought as I stood there, all of this is rather wasted on a dog.

For instead of Byron's grave, this is the burial spot of Boatswain, his adored Newfoundland who died aged five in November 1808, from rabies. As the melancholic Byron wrote to a friend: 'Boatswain is dead! – he expired in a state of madness on the 18th, after suffering much, yet retaining all the gentleness of his nature to the last, never attempting to do the least injury to anyone near him. I have now lost everyone except old Murray.' This was a reference to his old servant, whose first name was Joe and who, along with Boatswain, was supposed to share Byron's grave.

The idea, as set out in his will of 1811, was for Byron to be buried, his tombstone stating only his name and age, with the dog under the monument at Newstead. Also designated to join them underground was Joe, though apparently he objected to being buried with a dog. Actually, as Joe must have known, it could have been much worse. Byron was quite animal mad, with a lifetime menagerie that included a fox, monkeys, parrot, cats, eagle, crocodile, falcon, peacocks, an Egyptian crane and a badger. Then there was the bear, not to mention the wolf. When Byron went to Trinity College, Cambridge in 1805 the rules forbade him from keeping Boatswain. So he promptly installed a tame bear in his rooms (the rules not mentioning ursines).

After Trinity, Byron trundled back, along with the bear, to Newstead, where they were reunited with the wolf. It seems that one of Byron's ancestors at Newstead had kept a tame wolf and this was one of its descendants, a 'wolf dog' named Lyon. A Byron houseguest in 1809, Charles Skinner Matthews, claimed that 'playing with the bear or teasing the wolf' were regular amusements. At this time Byron had two Newfoundlands, or Newfies. One was Boatswain, as beautiful as his master, if the painting of him at Newstead is anything to go by. The other dog may have been called Thunder, who was larger but not as courageous as, apparently, he could seldom be induced to face the bear. And here's one more oddity, courtesy of the perfectly named David Pugsley of the Northern Newfoundland Club of Great Britain, who writes that: 'DNA analysis has revealed some interesting information. In the days before photography, it was the custom for lovers to exchange a lock of their hair. Analysis of over 100 samples sent by Byron to his various fans and lovers shows that most of these came from a dog, in all probability, Boatswain.'

When Boatswain died, Byron was lucky not to follow, as while nursing the dog he had wiped the slaver from his lips. The deeply indebted poet promptly commissioned the lavish large monument, with marble slabs, which was placed over the tomb on the location of the former high altar. And, then, he wrote this and put it as an epitaph:

> Near this spot
> Are deposited the Remains of one
> Who possessed Beauty without Vanity,
> Strength without Insolence,
> Courage without Ferocity,
> And all the Virtues of Man without his Vices.
> This Praise, which would be unmeaning Flattery
> If inscribed over human ashes,
> Is but a just tribute to the Memory of
> BOATSWAIN, a DOG
> Who was born at Newfoundland, May, 1803,
> And died at Newstead, Nov 18th, 1808.

When some proud Son of Man returns to Earth,
Unknown by Glory, but upheld by Birth,
The sculptor's art exhausts the pomp of woe,
And storied urns record who rests below.
When all is done, upon the Tomb is seen,
Not what he was, but what he should have been.
But the poor Dog, in life the firmest friend,
The first to welcome, foremost to defend,
Whose honest heart is still his master's own,
Who labours, fights, lives, breathes for him alone,
Unhonour'd falls, unnotic'd all his worth,
Deny'd in heaven the Soul he held on earth:

While man, vain insect! hopes to be forgiven,
And claims himself a sole exclusive heaven.
Oh man! thou feeble tenant of an hour,
Debas'd by slavery, or corrupt by power,
Who knows thee well, must quit thee with disgust,
Degraded mass of animated dust!
Thy love is lust, thy friendship all a cheat,
Thy tongue hypocrisy, thy heart deceit,
By nature vile, ennobled but by name,
Each kindred brute might bid thee blush for shame.
Ye! Who behold perchance this simple urn,
Pass on, it honours none you wish to mourn:
To mark a friend's remains these stones arise;
I never knew but one – and here he lies.

The monument is the only piece of building work that Byron commissioned at Newstead, which was sold in 1817 to pay his debts. By then he was notorious for his lifestyle (a word that should have been invented for him). He was the original 'mad, bad and dangerous to know' scoundrel, the king of scandal, his exploits including an affair with Lady Caroline Lamb, rumours of incest with his half-sister Augusta and an unhappy marriage in 1815 to Lady Caroline's cousin, who left him after giving birth to their child, August Ada (more of whom later). The separation swirled with tales of violence, infidelity, sodomy and incest.

Given all that, Byron chose the far more peaceful option of going into exile and, eventually, to war. This is how he died, of fever, during the fight for Greek independence, at the age of thirty-seven, in the town of Missolonghi. The Greeks shut offices and shops for days and wore black for three weeks. Byron lay in state and there was even a suggestion that he should be interred at the summit of the Parthenon. If only! Sadly, for him, he was returned to England, accompanied on the good ship *Florida* by another Newfie, Lyon (no relation to the wolf).

In England, it seems that reports of his death led to Princess Diana-esque eruptions of public shock and dismay. Newspapers which had pilloried him in life, fêted him in death. 'Thus has perished,' thundered the *Morning Chronicle*, 'the flower of his age, in the noblest of causes, one of the greatest poets England ever produced.' But Westminster Abbey and St Paul's had longer memories. The flower of his age was found morally wanting and was denied burial.* So Byron was sent home, to Nottinghamshire, but not to join Boatswain, for Newstead's new owners didn't want Byron either. It was the family vault in the nearby town of Hucknall for him.

What a peculiar funeral cortège it was that left London. The first hearse contained the coffin, the following coach was said to carry vases containing his internal organs (removed during autopsy and there are reports that some, the heart in particular, stayed in Greece). Many of the coaches that followed were empty, their owners having hit on the marvellous wheeze of 'ghost' appearances as a way of paying tribute to Byron without being seen personally to condone his behaviour. In Nottingham, people queued for four days to view the coffin and there were mob scenes at the funeral at St Mary Magdalene Church in Hucknall.

These days, Hucknall is a town that has seen better times. The first tribute that I saw to the great man was a sign on a giant multiplex: 'Welcome to the Byron Bingo: Doors Open at 6 p.m.' Its town centre seems a soulless place. The church is next to a litter-strewn car park with some ugly, if functioning, toilets. It was only when I looked up, over the shops with recycled furniture in their windows on Ogle Street, that I found

---

* The plaque now in Westminster Abbey was placed there in 1969.

him. There, looking out from a recessed arch, is a white statue of Byron: refined, dandified, glorious, looking preposterously out of place. In the shrubs around the graveyard, empty lager cans acted as embellishments, tinny flowers of our age.

The church was locked (of course) when I was there. His daughter Ada Lovelace, who never met him, chose to be buried with him, filling Boatswain's place. In the graveyard, if you hunt round long enough, you'll find a tribute to her as an 'enchantress of numbers'. An extraordinary mathematician, she collaborated with Charles Babbage, the inventor of the 'difference machine' that would become the world's first computer. Thus Byron's daughter is often called the first computer programmer.

Creepily, even in death, there was no peace for Byron. In 1938, Hucknall having been a place of pilgrimage, the vicar, worried by rumours that Byron wasn't really there at all, gained permission from the Home Office to open the coffin. This was his report: 'Reverendly, very reverendly, I raised the lid, and before my eyes lay the embalmed body of Byron, in as perfect a condition as when it had been placed in the coffin 114 years ago.' The churchwarden (the re-opening had an audience of forty!) couldn't resist adding his comments that the 'sexual organ showed quite abnormal development' and that Byron's deformed foot wasn't attached at all but was 'detached from his leg and lay at the bottom of his coffin'. Yikes.

I roamed round the rather dreary graveyard. Surely there would be some beauty here. Surely the poet who wrote

She walks in beauty, like the night
Of cloudless climes and starry skies

would be given something in acknowledgement of what he had given us? And I did find, outside one door to the church,

a memorial in the shape of an open book. It is black stone. On
the left hand page it says in flowing script: 'Byron, 1788–1824'.
On the next are these lines from *Childe Harold's Pilgrimage*:

BUT THERE IS THAT WITHIN ME WHICH SHALL TIRE
TORTURE AND TIME, AND BREATHE WHEN I EXPIRE.

In the crease lay one red rose. It did not seem enough.

# THE HANCOCK FAMILY:
## JOHN, FATHER, AND CHILDREN ELIZABETH, JOHN, ONER, WILLIAM, ALICE, ANN

### PLAGUE VICTIMS
### All dead in August 1666
*Off Riley Lane, just outside Eyam in Derbyshire*

## CATHERINE MOMPESSON

### VICAR'S WIFE
### Died 25 August 1666
*St Lawrence Church, Church Street, Eyam, Hope Valley,*
*Derbyshire S32 5QH*

On the eastern edge of the village of Eyam, pronounced Eem, up a track that winds its way through some trees, there comes on your left an open field with a stunning view of the Derbyshire countryside. Swallows swoop, the grass is so green that it almost glows. And, huddled together like a flock of sheep in the middle of the field, are seven graves.

Inside a stone enclosure, six small headstones bear the names of the Hancock children and their dates of burial in 1666: Elizabeth and John, on 3 August, Oner and William on 7 August, Alice on 9 August and, the next day, Ann. They are grouped around their father's tomb: a raised tomb with a large broken, lichened, worn, rectangular top. With difficulty, you can decipher this underneath the name John Hancock:

REMEMBER MAN

AS THOU GOEST BY

AS THOUGH ART NOW

EVEN SO WAS I

AS I DOE NOW

SO MUST THOU LYE

REMEMBER MAN

THAT THOU SHALT DIE

And die they certainly did in Eyam. These are the Riley Graves which tell the tale of one family all but destroyed in a village that was, itself, all but destroyed by the great plague – or 'the memorable woe' – of 1666. But, and this is the twist that fascinates, they died so that others could live. The story of Eyam is a tale that, today, still inspires something quite close to wonderment.

The plague had arrived here, in the bodies of fleas found in a damp bundle of cloth from London. The tailor's assistant who opened the bundle was dead within a week, on 7 September 1665. Many would follow but often, in a month, the toll would be only four or six. But when, in June 1666, nineteen out of a population of 300 expired, the vicar, the Reverend William Mompesson, came up with an extraordinary proposal: the village should quarantine itself with the aim of stopping the spread of the plague to other places in the North. No one could leave. Every family must bury their dead on their own land and not in the graveyard. Church services would be in the open. Food and clothing would be dropped on the village outskirts at what was called the Boundary Stone. It would be picked up at separate times. Payment would be made in coins that would be disinfected in vinegar.

It seems unbelievable that this plan worked. Even those who could flee, like the vicar's wife Catherine, stayed to what, she and others must have known, would be near certain death. She attained near saint-like status as she tended the sick. Both she and her husband must have asserted an incredible influence of almost cult-like proportions to get them to stay, and obey. Today, such a thing would never be allowed, by central government, by law, by us.

The plague, as William Mompesson knew it would, savaged Eyam, the toll climbing into three figures with many households wiped out. But, up that track, a half mile out of town, near what was known as the Riley slate pit, the Hancocks must have thought they had escaped. They had only one other family close by, the Talbots, who were blacksmiths. But, in July, plague came to the Talbots house and, by the end of July, ten adults and children had died. The only surviving members were the oldest among them, Bridget, aged seventy-eight, and her great grandchild, a three-month-old baby.

Imagine being Bridget, the last adult in the pest house, caring for the baby and also charged with digging the final graves. Wouldn't she have asked her neighbours for help? Or, perhaps, did they offer? Or feel they could not refuse? Is this how the plague came to the Hancocks' house? For the first Hancock child died on 3 August and, over the next week, Elizabeth, their mother, buried all six of her children and her husband in the field behind their house. A history of the village written by John Clifford notes: 'Each day that week, as the people of Stoney Middleton, in the valley far below, trudged to the boundary stone with their supplies of food, they saw Mrs Hancock at her melancholy task.'

Did these three now live together? If so, it would have been three generations in one pest house. But Elizabeth Hancock would next bury Bridget, on 15 August, and then, finally, the baby, in the field near the Talbot house. Now, alone, with only graves for comfort, Elizabeth did the unthinkable – she fled, going to Sheffield, where her one remaining son was apprenticed to a cutler. She did not, apparently, carry the plague. Extraordinarily, she was one of just two who left the village. (There was also, reportedly, someone who tried to come in!)

Back in the village proper, Catherine Mompesson is known

for having worked tirelessly with her husband, visiting the sick and dying. In his book, Mr Clifford explains that one of the symptoms of plague was a rather sickly sweet cloying sensation in the nostrils. One evening in August 1666, as she and her husband were returning to the rectory across the fields after hours of work, she is said to have exclaimed: 'How sweet the air smells.' That sentence filled her husband with alarm.

She died on what is believed to have been 25 August and is buried in a raised tomb, the only known plague grave in the churchyard. At the foot is an hourglass, with extended wings, cut into the stone with the inscription: 'CAVETE: NESCITIS: HORAM' (Beware, ye know not the hour). On the opposite side are the words 'MORS: MIHI: LVCRVM' (Death is my gain). At the end of August, every year, a wreath of red flowers is laid on it.

The plague stopped in October 1666, as quickly as it had begun. In November, the vicar wrote to a friend: 'The condition of the place has been so sad that I persuade myself it did not exceed all history and example. Our town has become a Golgotha – the place of a skull; and had there not been a small remnant left we had been as Sodom and like Gomorrah. My ears never heard such doleful lamentations, my nose never smelled such horrid smells and my eyes never beheld such ghastly spectacles.'

The village of Eyam is now picturesque, the plague houses lining up in a neat row next to the impressive parish church. There is even a museum for the plague tourists. The churchyard includes a gorgeous eighth-century Anglo-Saxon stone cross. Those who walk up to the Riley Graves, now taken care of by the National Trust, will be struck by the sheer beauty of the place with the plunging patchwork landscape of the Peak District spread out below. 'Sacred to the memory of the Hancock family,' says a plaque on the rough stone wall. 'Treat this burial place with reverence.'

# SIR STANLEY MATTHEWS

## FOOTBALLER
### 1 February 1915–23 February 2000
*Britannia Stadium, Sir Stanley Matthews Way,*
*Stoke-on-Trent ST4 4EG*

His funeral, it is said, after royalty and Winston Churchill, was the biggest that modern England has seen. An estimated 100,000 people came out onto the wet and windy streets of Stoke to pay their respects to the man they called 'The Wizard', who was born in a terraced house here, the son of a boxer, and then dribbled his way to fame. The cortège, nine vehicles with police escorts, started inside the hilltop Britannia Stadium and then wound its way for fourteen miles, over roundabouts and small brick streets, past his birthplace in Hanley and his primary school, to St Peter's Church. The pavements were lined, ten to twelve feet deep, with people, a river of red and white (Stoke colours). The leading hearse was decked with red roses and white carnations in the shape of a football shirt with his number seven. The family had asked for no flowers but hundreds of bouquets were left outside the stadium where, after the funeral, Sir Stan's ashes were buried under the pitch.

John Ezard wrote a marvellous piece on the day in *The Guardian*. He noted:

The note of wonder and informality continued in church, where the first hymn listed was 'And Did Those Feet?', usually called Blake's 'Jerusalem', and the second, chosen by Matthews' family, was 'Lord of the Dance'. Many of the 300 fans who were given a third of the church seats draped Stoke City scarves over their gallery balcony. The watchword of the day was respect. Cheers began in a few throats and a few fists punched the air. But these gestures were choked off by the collective mood of the crowds. Instead, there was applause. It started in the cortège's journey of honour through the three-year-old £14.7 million stadium, on an exposed hill above the towns. Hands were at first too cold to clap loudly or without pain. But they persisted and warmed into the first of a series of great, solemn, minutes-long ovations of respect which were repeated wherever the motorcade travelled on its 75-minute tour.

It is hard now, in an age when footballers are made of gold, as in money, to remember the age when they were simply golden. Sir Stan is said to have made 710 appearances, played for Stoke and Blackpool, won fifty-four England caps and was never booked. Playing at a time of the maximum wage of £5 a week, he was never rich – or rude. A former teammate Jimmy Armfield said at his funeral, 'He was often kicked and fouled but he never retaliated. Despite his global fame, he was very much a man of the people.' Stoke City chairman Peter Coates described him as friendly and modest, a man who never criticised players. 'This city had master potter Josiah Wedgwood, literary figure Arnold Bennett, Victorian scientist Oliver Lodge and *Spitfire* designer Reginald Mitchell. But nobody played the same part in the lives of people in this city as Stan. He was a working-class hero.'

'Proud to be a Potter' waves the banner attached to the side of massive bowl on a hill that is the Britannia stadium. In the front, overlooking what had been Victoria Ground, where he had played, there is a massive plinth, on which are three nine-foot statues of Sir Stanley in motion: first at the start of his career, then as a England International and, finally, at the end of his career (he didn't retire until his fifties). The shirts, shorts, boots and balls are all copied from the authentic articles. I was there on a bitterly cold day. You can book a tour of the stadium, by the way, where you can see the Stanley Matthews room. I was joined, in front of the statue, by a young family with a boy of five or six who would not stop kicking his football at the base.

## SIR MAURICE OLDFIELD

### SPY
### 16 November 1915–11 March 1981
*St Anne's Churchyard, Main Street, Over Haddon,*
*Derbyshire DE45 1JE*

'So,' said the taxi driver, apropos nothing, as we drove through the Derbyshire countryside. 'Do you know who is buried in the churchyard at Over Hadden?'

I did not know. Nor did I know how the taxi driver could possibly know that I would be interested. But I knew enough not to say this and simply ask who it could be.

'The head of MI6,' said the taxi driver. 'Maurice Oldfield. He's got a lot of letters after his name.'

And so, the next day, we paid a visit to St Anne's at Over Hadden, a small village a few miles from the market town of Bakewell in the Peak District National Park in Derbyshire. There, on a slope, overlooking the beautiful Lathkill Dale, were the headstones of what seemed like dozens of Oldfields, all similar, weathered, rounded, the letters invaded by lichen and the stone faded by the weather. But, eventually, I found the right one: 'Maurice Oldfield GCMG CBE, who died 11 March 1981, aged sixty-six, eldest son of Joseph and Annie Oldfield'. His sister, Irene, is also on the gravestone.

It is the perfect grave for the man who, enigmatic and retiring, would be known as 'C', who was in the secret services for thirty-two years, who was posted to Washington during the Kennedy assassination. In announcing his death, *The Times* claimed he was the model for the legendary Smiley in John le Carré's novels and 'M' in Ian Fleming's James Bond books. While le Carré always denied this, he does tell the story that Sir Alec Guinness, upon discovering he was to play Smiley in *Tinker Tailor Soldier Spy*, asked him if he could introduce him to the real deal. 'So I rang Sir Maurice Oldfield,' says le Carré. 'He said, "Oh yes. I'd love to. I'm a great admirer of Sir Alec." Alec then rang me and said: "What shall I wear? Something very very grey?"'

I feel almost guilty putting Maurice Oldfield among my 100, so complete is the modest obscurity of this grave. But there was nothing ordinary about the man, the most sophisticated of spies, acknowledged as a 'gleaming legend' of the intelligence world. That he should come from here, one of eleven children of a tenant farmer, was even more extraordinary. He went on to Manchester University where he got an Honours First, specialising in the medieval clergy, of all things. This could have been his life – except that he then enlisted.

'He is the best counter-intelligence officer, both from the theoretical and practical point of view, that it has been my privilege to meet. He is quite outstanding,' said Brigadier Roberts, in charge of Field Security in the Middle East during the Second World War. After the war Maurice joined MI6, working his way up the ranks, both at home and abroad, until, in 1973, he got the top job, the first insider to be promoted to it. What is interesting, reading up about him, is that he was apparently quite unaffected by all of this. 'His modesty was genuine and his charm natural,' said *The Times* in their obit in 1981.

He had a penchant for telling stories and apparently one of his favourites was about a retired MI6 officer who had become a prison visitor. He met a prisoner convicted of burglary who told him that he had once done some (legitimate) repair work at the MI6 offices. He had 'cased the joint' but remarked that it must be a very queer organisation because people did not talk to each other in the lifts and they left nothing on their desks. 'Nothing worth nickin' there, guv'r,' the prisoner summarised. And Maurice Oldfield always said that if he ever wrote his autobiography: 'Nothing worth nickin' would be the title. But he didn't write an autobiography. Of course.

# ANTHONY E. PRATT

## BOARD GAME INVENTOR
### 10 August 1903–9 April 1994
*Old Bromsgrove Cemetery, Church Lane, Bromsgrove,*
*Worcestershire B61 8RB*

It seems appropriate, for reasons you will soon find out, that this story begins with a body and a mystery. So here's the body. It belongs to Anthony Pratt and he lies in Bromsgrove Cemetery, in section 2B, near the laburnum tree. The tombstone says: 'Inventor of Cluedo'. There were red roses. 'A Very Dear Father', it adds. 'Sadly missed.' It was immediately intriguing. Anthony Pratt should have been rich and famous – fêted and celebrated as the inventors of Monopoly are – but instead he died ordinary and forgotten in 1994. What happened? And that is the mystery.

I visited this grave for the first time years ago, for an article I wrote for *The Independent* which was prompted by a small item I had read somewhere about how the company Waddingtons had lost touch with the inventor of the world's second most popular board game, which has also spawned a film, a stage play and a TV series. In 1996, on the occasion of the 150 millionth game sold, Waddingtons had set up a 'Cluedo hotline' to obtain information on Mr Pratt. 'Wanted: For Murder Most Enjoyable', said the press release. But by then, Mr Pratt was already in his grave, having spent his last years suffering from Alzheimer's in an old peoples' home.

I tracked down his daughter, Marcia Davies, a senior civil servant in Birmingham. She was the only child of Anthony and Elva Pratt and, as such, the sole living link to the history of Cluedo. The epitaph was her idea. 'We never talked about it but I thought for purposes of posterity, it seemed right,' she told me. I visited Birmingham Central Library but was met with puzzlement. 'Never heard of him,' said the librarian. 'Funny name, Pratt. What did you say he did? Cluedo. Hmmmm.' In the end, we did find one small article, with a short interview.

Anthony Pratt was born with a talent for music and, after leaving school, he played the piano for a living, touring as part of an orchestra on ocean liners. He enjoyed life and his hobbies, particularly reading, more than work. He had a large book collection and was partial to books on crime and psychology. He also liked parties and particularly a party game called Murder, where guests crept up on each other and victims shrieked and fell over. During the Second World War, he worked at a factory in Birmingham. The black-out meant no parties – or games of Murder. In a 1990 interview (found in the library), he said: 'I was leaning on the fence of our King's Heath home and it dawned on me that this wretched old war was killing the country's social life.' On the other side of the fence was his friend, Geoffrey Bull, who had invented the high-seas adventure game Buccaneer and sold it to Waddingtons. This inspired Mr Pratt to invent his own murder mystery game.

After our interview, Marcia Davies went home and looked in an unopened box of her father's papers. There she found the original game. It was called 'Murder!' and was set in an unnamed country house. There were ten characters, one of which was chosen to be the victim of each game. These were: Dr Black, Mr Brown, Mr Gold, the Rev. Green, Miss Grey, Professor Plum, Miss Scarlet, Nurse White, Mrs Silver and Colonel Yellow. The nine weapons were: axe, cudgel, bomb, rope, dagger, revolver, hypodermic syringe, a bottle of poison and a poker. The original board was drawn by Elva.

The Pratts demonstrated the game to Waddingtons in Leeds in 1945. A few changes were made. The house was named Tudor Hall. There would be only six characters and the Colonel would have to be called Mustard. The bomb was rejected, a candlestick (much more country home) substituted. The syringe was replaced with a bit of lead piping. The board, as drawn by Elva, was not altered. The game was renamed Cluedo (combining Clue and Ludo, a Latin word for play). In 1947, Anthony Pratt was granted a patent. An agreement was signed with Waddingtons and production began in 1949.

Success was elusive. 'In 1952 and 1953, Waddingtons wrote that sales were not going too well,' said Marcia Davies. 'In May 1953, my father signed over all royalties, in respect of overseas sales, for £5,000.' This, then, was the big mistake. Cluedo, or Clue, as it is in the States, would end up selling millions in twenty-three countries. If Anthony Pratt had even the tiniest of slivers of the overseas sales, he would have died very rich indeed. But, in those days, £5,000 wasn't exactly chicken feed. They moved to Bournemouth and bought a large house with holiday flats. The British patent was extended until 1965. Some quarters he would receive a large cheque, other times it would be only a few hundred. 'And my wife would lament that we weren't Americans who'd have made a fortune,' he said in his 1990 interview. In his papers, there were two other games that he had submitted to Waddingtons without success, one centred on buried treasure, the other on a gold mine. Eventually the cheques dwindled to the point where he went back to work as a solicitor's clerk.

Looking back, in 1990, he seemed sanguine. 'A letter came with a cheque and the news that there would be no more because the patents had lapsed. That was that. We did not mind, you know. It had been one of life's bonuses. A great deal of fun went into it. So why grumble?' Except, of course, at home, there were some grumbles. Their game, the board that Elva had drawn, the characters that Anthony had invented, was an international superstar. But they were living in Birmingham in obscurity and relative austerity. So that's their story and my mystery, at least, has been solved.

# RICHARD III

## KING OF ENGLAND
### 2 October 1452–22 August 1485
*Leicester Cathedral (or that's the plan), St Martin's House,*
*7 Peacock Lane, Leicester LE1 5PZ*

'**M**y grave, my grave, my kingdom for a grave.' That, surely, would be Richard III's lament ever since he was discovered by University of Leicester archaeologists to be lurking beneath a council car park on the site of what had been Greyfriars monastery. Richard was buried there after being killed at the Battle of Bosworth Field, the decisive battle of the War of the Roses. The skeleton had ten wounds, eight to the head, an arrow in the spine and scoliosis. DNA evidence confirmed what seemed rather obvious: this was the body of Richard III. The Ministry for Justice ruled the king should get a funeral and this news, at Westminster, unleashed its very own War of the Poses. MPs couldn't wait to give their idea of where he should be buried with the list including Barnard Castle, Worksop and York.

And of course, Leicester. That city's MP Jonathan Ashworth noted that since Richard III had been lying under it for 500 years, then he should stay in the city.

Hugh Bayley, from York, pointed out that it wasn't 500 years but 527. 'Despite that passage of time, he is still very well regarded in York,' he noted.

'Is he still on the electoral roll?' asked one Labour MP.

It seems that the powers that be have decided that Richard III will remain in Leicester, though York battles on through the courts. There was a panicky moment when Mr Ashworth thought the government might be U-turning on the king. This sounded painful though surely, for Richard III, being reversed over is nothing compared to eight blows to the head. Plus, as someone under a car park, he's seen his fair share of U-turns. This had another MP chanting: 'A hearse, a hearse, my kingdom for a hearse.'

So I headed off to Leicester in search of the car park. I have to tell you, there is no shortage of them there, even in the cathedral district. My first attempt had me pulling into a car park in New Street which, as it turned out, was just across the road from The Royal Car Park, which surely will be in danger of being renamed the Richard III Ye Olde Car Park. It was hidden behind green metal doors, topped by a metre of spiked railings. 'No public access,' said a sign next to another one that says 'Drive Slow'. I am sure that, at some point, the Royal Car Park will be part of the Richard III 'experience', but not quite yet.

Across the street is the cathedral itself, which isn't very grand. It used to be St Martin's church but was 'reordered' in 1927. There was already a memorial slab for Richard III in the cathedral but now it is raising money for what has been decided will be a raised stone tomb. There are plans for a memorial service and some sort of lying in state. There is also a promise that the cathedral will not start to charge entry for those who come to see the final resting place of the last Plantagenet king. Already, Richard III's face is everywhere here, on banners, on brochures, on doors. For Leicester, this is a tourist bonanza. For Richard III, I'm not so sure that he wouldn't prefer his quiet old car park.

*Eleanor Rigby, St Peter's Churchyard, Woolton, Liverpool*

# THE NORTH

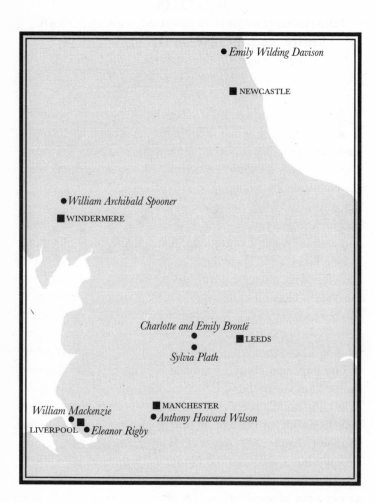

# CHARLOTTE AND EMILY BRONTË

## WRITERS
**Charlotte (21 April 1816–31 March 1855) and
Emily (30 July 1818–19 December 1848)**
*St Michael and All Angels Church, Church Street,
Haworth, West Yorkshire BD2 28DR*

Haworth is always called a village but it is actually a suburb and a busy one at that. The Parsonage Museum, which was the home of the Brontë sisters for forty-one years, is at the top of a hill, very near the church in which Charlotte and Emily were buried. (Anne, the youngest, is in Scarborough.) This is one of the graves that I had to include in my 100 by popular demand because so many people asked if I had been to Haworth. I never had and so I went. I must admit that I found the whole scene to be a bit of a zoo. I climbed the pedestrianised hill up to the church and parsonage, past the Ye Olde Brontë Tea-Rooms and the Villette Coffee House, not to mention Spooks bookshop. It was hot and, outside the Black Bull pub, there was way too much flesh on show. I stood and looked down the hill at the tat and the bunting. Could there be a scene that could be less Brontëan?

The imposing church has been rebuilt since the Brontës' time. They were buried in a vault near their old pew. Emily, the middle sister and author of *Wuthering Heights*, died first, from TB, at the age of thirty. The next to go was the youngest, Anne (*The Tenant of Wildfell Hall*) at the age of twenty-nine. Charlotte, the author of *Jane Eyre*, lasted until thirty-nine. Their deaths seem tragic now but, at the time, 41 per cent of children in Haworth died before they were six. Today that world seems light-years away. Haworth is a hubbub of tourism and I was in the church with dozens of others. Behind the church is a graveyard, which is lovely now, a respite from the bustle, but, in the Brontës' time, was badly

drained not to mention overcrowded. Two of their serv-
ants, Tabby Ackroyd and Martha Brown, are buried here.
The graveyard backs onto glorious countryside, the moors
so beloved of the sisters though, on this summer day, they
hardly looked dark and brooding. It was way too sunny for
Heathcliff, a man who never felt the desire to work on his tan.

This place is redeemed, however, by The Parsonage
Museum. Here, inside, you can begin to see – and feel – how
the world's most famous literary family lived. There is not only
room for tourists in Haworth but pilgrims and serious Brontë
devotees too. And this is what brought Patti Smith, inimitable
songstress, and her sister Linda here in April 2013: they are
big Brontë fans and even read *Villette* to each other every day
at one point. ('When it comes to literature,' says Patti, 'I like
a girl's story.') Patti did an interview with the BBC from The
Parsonage itself. 'Most of the Brontës passed away here,' she
says. 'They did their work here, wrote masterpieces here, expe-
rienced so much beauty and tragedy here. It's quite moving.'

What, asked the BBC reporter, had Patti learned from her
visit? She replied:

I don't think about it as learning. It's more experiencing.
Proximity means quite a bit to me. Some people don't understand
that. I find proximity very moving, to walk on the floorboards
where Charlotte walked or sit at the chair where she sat, or be
in a room, and the atmosphere where so much happened. Each
room contains its joys and sorrows, which is like life. The joys
and sorrows of such extraordinary people, really.

After Haworth, Patti and her sister were heading to St Mary's
Church in Scarborough to see Anne's grave (she had travelled
there in search of fresh air and better health but her trip was
in vain). 'It's quite a pilgrimage,' says Patti, 'a happy pilgrimage with my sister, we are overjoyed to be here.'

# EMILY WILDING DAVISON

## SUFFRAGETTE AND MARTYR
## 11 October 1872–8 June 1913
*St Mary the Virgin Churchyard, Morpeth,*
*Northumberland NE61 2QT*

There is some irony in the fact that the Bible verse chosen for Emily Wilding Davison's grave is from John: 'Greater love hath no man than this, that a man lay down his life for his friends.' Because, of course, Emily was not a man but a woman and a supremely angry one at that. She sacrificed her life, or certainly risked doing so, when she ran out in front of the King's horse at Epsom, not for friends but for a radical political cause, votes for women. She was a militant, an arsonist, a violent campaigner who had, among other things, launched an attack on Chancellor David Lloyd George. She was imprisoned nine times, each time going on hunger strike, suffering force-feeding. But also, under the Bible verse from John, on the tall white monument in the quiet Morpeth churchyard, is her epitaph: 'Deeds not words'. There is no irony there, only power.

Emily is now a legend but the truth is that, if she were to do the same things today as then, she would be seen as something quite close to a terrorist. Who knows what she would have become if she had lived in later, better times? Perhaps an MP, though of course she didn't have that option. She was a teacher and raised enough money to study Biology, Chemistry and English at St Hugh's College, Oxford where she would have obtained a first class honours degree if women were allowed to have such things then. She joined Emmeline Pankhurst's militant Women's Social and Political Union movement in 1906 and, in 1908, quit her teaching job to devote herself to the suffragette cause. Determined.

Courageous. Fearless. She was, in the end, banned from the Palace of Westminster. But if you go down into St Mary's Undercroft, the chapel that lies below the vast and ancient Westminster Hall, behind the organ, you would find a little broom cupboard. This is where she hid overnight on 1 April 1911 in order to be able to record her residence at the House of Commons in the Census. There is a plaque on the back of the door, above which is a picture of Emily, commemorating this. It ends: 'By such means was democracy won for the people of Britain.'

It is generally believed now that Emily Wilding Davison had no intention of committing suicide when she bought a (return) ticket to Epsom on 4 June 1913. But, certainly, she intended to disrupt proceedings when she headed out onto the track as the horse Anmer owned by King George V raced by. Mary Richardson, who was with her on the day and herself held up a copy of *The Suffragette*, said she wasn't nervous.

> A minute before the race started she raised a paper of her own or some kind of card before her eyes. I was watching her hand. It did not shake. Even when I heard the pound of the horses' hooves moving close, I saw she was still smiling. And suddenly she slipped under the rail and ran out into the middle of the racecourse. It was all over so quickly.

She was thrown to the ground by the horse, and trampled. She died four days later in hospital from a fractured skull. It is now thought that her intention was to tie a WSPU scarf, in the suffragette colours of green and purple, to the horse's bridle. There were huge crowds at her memorial service and funeral and it is pleasing to see, tied to the railings that surround her pristine monument, some trailing green and purple ribbons. Deeds, not words, indeed.

# WILLIAM MACKENZIE

## RAILWAY ENGINEER AND GHOST
### 20 March 1794–29 October 1851
*St Andrew's Graveyard, Rodney Street, Liverpool L1 2TQ*

It was a dark and stormy night when, through the gloom, I saw it – the haunted pyramid of Rodney Street, a 15ft granite edifice. OK, so it was actually an unusually warm day in mid-September some years ago, but still, it *was* spooky as I stopped and peered at the pyramid, through the metal fence that surrounded the overgrown graveyard of the long disused St Andrew's Church. A plaque in the middle of the pyramid looked just like an eye, staring right back at me, as if it knew I was looking.

I soon learned it was the grave of one William Mackenzie, an engineer who built railways and canals around the British Isles and in France, Spain, Belgium and in the Italian states. But not, sadly, Egypt, for it would make this story complete. He was a successful man, and when he died at the age of fifty-seven he left most of his £341,848 estate to his brother

Edward. There is an inscription on the pyramid, Grade II listed, which identifies it as William Mackenzie's grave and ends: 'The memory of the just is blessed.'

But forget the memory of the just. What we are concerned with here is the memory of the unjust, if not downright wicked. For decades, and probably centuries, the pyramid has inspired those who love a good ghost story. And so, for illumination, I turn to the *Fortean Times*, experts on all such things. Legend has it that William Mackenzie was a gambler who insisted that he be buried sitting upright, holding a winning hand of cards. The Devil had said he would only take his soul once he was laid to rest in a grave. So Mackenzie, by staying above ground, was the winner.

There are two stories as to how Mackenzie met the Devil. One is that he asked Satan to help him win a card game and Satan agreed, in exchange for his soul. The second is that Mackenzie became an atheist following the early death of his wife (and his first wife, who is also in the pyramid, did die aged forty-eight). He took up a life of drinking and gambling and one night he met his match at the poker table, in the form of a mysterious man named Mr Madison. Mackenzie lost all his money but Madison asked him if he would play one last hand.

'But I have nothing left,' said Mr Mackenzie.

'What about your soul?' asked Mr Madison.

Mackenzie refused, realising he was being tempted by the Devil himself. But then Madison, who knew a thing or two about winning an argument, said that surely, as an atheist, Mackenzie would not believe in the existence of a soul anyway. So what's to lose? So Mackenzie agreed – and lost. At this point Madison said he would take his soul when he was dead and buried, and vanished.

How do we know this? It seems that one dark and stormy night, a Rodney Street doctor met Mackenzie's ghost

– complete with top hat and flapping black coat – who told him about the pact that he'd made with the Devil. It is said that Mackenzie continues to haunt the graveyard, though now he's got new neighbours with St Andrew's having recently been converted into student flats.

But what of the pyramid itself? Does it give any clues? Facing the street is a small blind entrance, and over it a lintel with a plaque. The inscription explains that the pyramid was built by Edward 'as a token of love and affection' in 1868 – i.e. seventeen years after his brother died. It also says that William Mackenzie lies in the vault beneath the pyramid. So maybe not sitting up after all. Still, the Devil is in the detail and it's a great story.

## SYLVIA PLATH

**POET**
**27 October 1932–11 February 1963**
*St Thomas the Apostle Graveyard, Church Street,*
*Heptonstall, West Yorkshire HX7 7NT*

.Iwas both fascinated and a little fearful of the idea of visiting Sylvia Plath's grave. I knew that it had become a place
of pilgrimage for admirers of her searing and fearless poetry.
But I also knew that it had been repeatedly defaced by those
who think her estranged husband and fellow poet, the now
late Ted Hughes, was responsible for her 1963 suicide in a
freezing flat in Fitzroy Square in London, when she left their
two young children locked in the bedroom with bread and
butter and glasses of milk, taping the door to protect them
from the gas. These women visited the grave to chisel off the
word 'Hughes' but, each time, he had the stone removed
and restored.

It had been one of those days when I visited. Roads had
been shut, the sat-nav appeared to be sending me to the
moon most of the time and, in the end, I found Heptonstall
by sheer accident. I was completely unprepared for the stark
beauty of this classic Yorkshire stone village, a former centre
for weaving that hugs the hill over Hebden Bridge for dear
life. The road up was so steep and narrow that I thought
I had made yet another mistake as I gunned my car up it:
surely, I thought, this could not be two-way (though it was).
For reasons unknown, I had always imagined Sylvia Plath's
grave in a valley, not here, virtually touching the sky.

I was also in a hurry, not to mention hot and bothered. But
rushing down the hill now, having finally found a place to
park, to find the church, I was overwhelmed to find that this
small place has two churches, the bleak imperious ruin that

is St Thomas à Becket, surrounded by tombstones, and its replacement, St Thomas the Apostle. I stopped outside the tiny village museum, open on this unseasonably hot Sunday afternoon in May. I looked out on what seemed a sea of graves and felt a sense of panic. How the hell was I ever going to find Sylvia here?

'Can I help you?' asked an older gentleman named John who sported a green blazer with a Queen's Own Rifle of Canada badge. Was that a pipe in his hand? Did people still smoke pipes?

Embarrassed, I said I was looking for Sylvia Plath's grave. 'I'll take you there,' he volunteered, chatting away about how he had married a girl from Heptonstall. He was from another village which I think was Mytholmroyd, Ted Hughes's birth-place, down in the valley below. John and his wife were now living in Canada and he returned once a year to visit friends. He chatted comfortably as we ambled past the swathe of old tombstones around the church and headed off towards another, far more modern graveyard.

'Poor Sylvia,' he said. 'You know there were only five at the funeral.'

Five? He nodded. 'I'm not sure if my mother-in-law played the organ for it,' he mused.

He guided me to the grave, in the third row back. The flowers were tousled and feminine, the grave bed a cloud of columbine and comfrey. There were many little stones on the tombstone itself and, in front of it, there was a fat pot of pens, something I have also seen on the grave of writer Douglas Adams in Highgate. The name is Sylvia Plath Hughes – 'The feminists haven't been round for a while,' says John – and, beside her dates, is the epitaph that Ted chose for her from the *Bhagavadgītā*: 'Even amidst fierce flames the golden lotus can be planted.'

I walked back with John, through the almost surreal

landscape of the ruined church. I could see other Sylvia pilgrims on their way to the grave. Hers is a much loved grave and her poetry is adored now. But when she died, her auto-biographical novel, *The Bell Jar*, had been published for only a month and her book of poetry, *Ariel*, was just a manuscript. It was published two years after her death. Her funeral was only attended by a handful though further research shows the number was more likely to be eight people, not five. There were, apparently, no immediate obituaries. But her memory has been one that certainly has haunted ever since. She will never be forgotten.

# ELEANOR RIGBY

## INSPIRATION AND SCULLERY MAID
### 1895 (day unknown)–10 October 1939
*St Peter's Churchyard, Church Road,*
*Woolton, Liverpool L25 6DA*

Eleanor Rigby died in the church and was buried along with
her name.

Nobody came.

Lyric from 'Eleanor Rigby', McCartney–Lennon, 1964

'Eleanor Rigby' is a song about loneliness but I can tell
you that, if she ever was lonely, except in the song,
then she's certainly not now. Her gravestone, near the church
where John Lennon and Paul McCartney met on the Saturday
evening of 6 July 1957, must be one of the most visited in the
country. Paul was fifteen when he was introduced to John,
aged sixteen, and other members of The Quarrymen during
a break at a church dance. The meeting was brief but Paul
was asked to join the group and the rest is history. When we
were there, on a blistering hot summer Monday afternoon,
there were two Beatles tour groups, one in Spanish, the other
in Scouse. They went to Eleanor's grave and also, round the
back of the church, to see the graves of John's uncle, George
Toogood Smith and legendary football manager Bob Paisley.
You'd be challenged to be lonely here.

The 1966 song, the B-side of 'Yellow Submarine', was
mostly written by Paul, who says that the original name
that came to him was Daisy Hawkins and that the name of
the priest who gave sermons that nobody heard was Father
McCartney but he didn't want people to think this was a
reference to his dad. Paul has claimed that he went through

the phone book to find Father McKenzie and that the name
Eleanor Rigby was a construct from the actress Eleanor Bron
and a store in Bristol. But, later, he conceded that the names
could easily have come from the graveyard where he and
John hung out. Paul even obtained a document with the real
Eleanor's signature on it.

There is no shortage of Rigbys at St Peter's. They are
all over the place. There's Ann and Alfred, Isabella and
Joseph. Even on Eleanor's stone (third row back as you
enter the main churchyard), are her grandparents John and
Frances and also a Doris, which may or may not have been
her daughter. And there is also another gravestone, in the
first row, with a Mr McKenzie (John). What little we know
about Eleanor Rigby has been pieced together by Beatles
researchers from basic records. We know, from the census,
that John and Frances had four children, among them Mary,
her mother, who married an Arthur Whitfield in 1893. Arthur
died, aged twenty-four, weeks after Eleanor was born, and
she and her mum moved back in with John and Frances.
Mary remarried when her daughter was fifteen, but Eleanor
seems to have taken against her step-father, refusing to take
his name. We know, thanks to a pay sheet discovered in 2008,
that she was a scullery maid at Liverpool City Hospital (it
was this bit of paper, which has her signature, that Paul
acquired and gave to charity to be auctioned off: it raised
£115,000). We also know that Eleanor married a man named
Thomas Woods and that she died aged forty-four. If Doris,
who died aged two, was her daughter, then she may have
been illegitimate.

From these facts, it is sometimes assumed that Eleanor
Rigby led a rather bleak life, similar to her namesake in the
song. But I really don't think the facts, scant as they are,
support this. Eleanor Rigby seems to have been surrounded

by family for all of her life, had a job and was, according to her gravestone, 'beloved' by her husband. She was working class, yes, but not lonely. She did not pick up the rice at the church where the wedding had been, living in a dream. I doubt she spent much time waiting at the window, wearing the face that she keeps in a jar by the door. And of this I am sure: there were people at her funeral. Still, it's a great song.

## WILLIAM ARCHIBALD SPOONER

### PROFESSOR AND SPOONERIST
#### 22 July 1844–29 August 1930
*Grasmere Cemetery, Pye Lane, Grasmere, Cumbria LA22 2AA*

Let me grow you to this shave, or even, if you insist, show you to this grave. It is in Grasmere, off the tourist track, well-trod by the hordes that come to visit another last resting place – that of William Wordsworth, in St Oswald's churchyard in the centre of this well-off Lake District village. I happened to visit Wordsworth on a Sunday and, what with the hymns wafting through the air, the smell of gingerbread from a nearby shop and the fact that it was daffodil season, it was pretty perfect. But, I have to tell you, no one at St Oswald's churchyard is wandering lonely as a cloud, though I accept that it would be possible to be wandering clone-ly as a loud. If you think that doesn't make sense, then you need to see the coach car park here.

Up the road (the A591) and turning off onto a (much) smaller lane you will find another cemetery, equally lovely and lonelier, in a good way. As you enter the gate, the path forks, so keep to the left: the grave, weathered now, is on the right, fourth row back, third stone in (plot 399). 'Manners maketh man', it says. This is the grave of William Archibald Spooner, cleric and scholar, fellow and Warden of New College, Oxford. It ends: 'Blessed are the peacemakers'. In the background, the hills do, I promise you, touch the clouds.

So here lies Dr Spooner, a short albino and 'rabbit-like' priest and faculty member, who lectured on Christianity, philosophy and ancient history. His was a moral life, devoted to his college, thoughtful, learned, courageous (after the First World War, he insisted that German students be listed along with the British ones on the college chapel war memorial).

He was beloved by his students, not least for his mistakes with the English language. It's not clear how often he actually transposed the start of his words. I suspect that the fact we call a spoonerism a spoonerism may be a very elongated student prank (prudent stank?). But there it is. That's what he became famous for. As he once scolded his students: 'You don't want to hear a speech, you just want me to say one of those ... things.'

So this list comes with a health warning, but they have been attributed to him: 'Kinquering congs their titles take', 'You have hissed all my mystery lectures' and 'You have deliberately tasted two worms'. Then there are these (probably made up by his students): 'The Lord is a shoving leopard' and 'It is kisstomary to cuss the bride'. He does seem to be the classic forgetful professor. One tale has him delivering a sermon about Aristotle to a baffled congregation. When he had finished, he went back up to the lectern to say: 'Did I say Aristotle? I meant St Paul.'

So here lies Dr Spooner, manners maketh man (no chance of spoonerism there). It seems that he lies in Grasmere because he and his wife used to holiday here in an old Victorian home called How Foot. It is now owned by the Wordsworth Trust and run as a bed and breakfast or, if you insist, bred and beakfast.

## ANTHONY HOWARD WILSON

### BROADCASTER AND MUSIC MOGUL
### 20 February 1950–10 August 2007
*Southern Cemetery, 212 Barlow Moor Road,*
*Chorlton-cum-Hardy, Manchester M21 7GL*

This is by far the coolest gravestone in this book. It was erected in 2010, three years late, which is apparently not that unusual for Peter Saville and Ben Kelly, designers for Factory, the record label that Tony Wilson founded in 1978. The only way to describe it is a work of art. It is a tall rectangle of black granite, so shiny and pure that, if you try and take a photo of it, you will find that you have a photograph of yourself reflected in the stone. It is enigmatic. In the top right hand corner is the name Anthony H. Wilson, which is the name he used to wind people up in Manchester who think 'I'm a flash twat'. He is described as a 'broadcaster' and 'cultural catalyst'. It sounds pretentious (moi?) but he was both, presenting numerous news and culture programmes for Granada and others and also founding the legendary Hacienda nightclub and, with Alan Erasmus, Factory Records, the home of Joy Division, New Order and the Happy Mondays. The dates are not cluttered by twiddly bits such as days or months. It sticks to years, 1950–2007, which is indeed so much cleaner.

In the bottom right-hand corner there is this quote:

Mutability is the epitaph of worlds
Change alone is changeless
People drop out of the history of life as of a land
Though their work or their influence remains.
*The Manchester Man*, G. Linnaeus Banks, 1876

The quotation, which was picked by his family, is from a novel written by Mrs G. Linnaeus Banks or Isabella Varley, which charts the life of Jabez Clegg (the eponymous Mr Manchester) from the Napoleonic Wars through to the first Reform Act, taking in the Peterloo Massacre and the Corn Law riots. It seems that the quotation is all about what Tony Wilson once called an 'excess of civic pride'. And, as you ask, I don't really understand it (yet) but you have to admit, it's interesting.

Tony Wilson once said: 'I am a minor player in my own life.' Yet when he died the flag flew at half-mast in Manchester. His coffin, underneath this work of art, was given a number, 501, as was everything in Factory Records, for not only art was seen as art there. (His book, the surreal *24 Hour Party People*, written as a companion to the film in which Wilson is played by Steve Coogan, is Factory Number 424.) When we were there, there were fresh roses and several lanterns. Plus, oddly, but again maybe it's just because I'm missing something, a watch showing the correct time.

This is a huge cemetery, well kept, easy to get around, the largest in the UK. The office is friendly and eager to help. There are many famous people buried here: Sir Matt Busby of Manchester United fame and the painter L. S. Lowry, whose grave, which he shares with his parents, has a jar of paintbrushes left by visitors. I chose Tony Wilson's grave because, even though I don't understand it, I know that *that*, probably, is the point. You don't have to understand something to love it.

*John Brown, Crathie Kirkyards, Crathie, Aberdeenshire*

# SCOTLAND

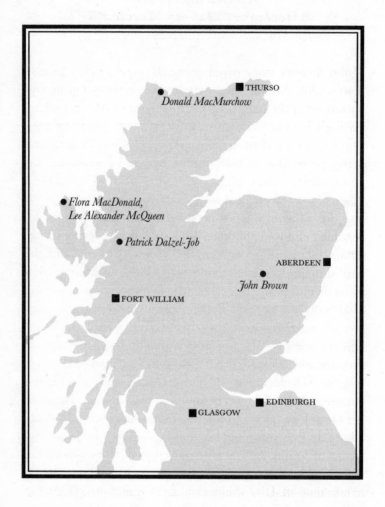

# JOHN BROWN

## ROYAL SERVANT
## 8 December 1826–27 March 1883
*Crathie Kirkyard, Crathie, Aberdeenshire AB35 5UL*

John Brown's story is not so much rags to riches as rags to royalty. Actually rags may be overdoing it, but he was born poor in the hamlet of Craithienaird in Aberdeenshire, leaving school at fourteen to work as a stable lad and then a ghillie, or outdoor servant. When Queen Victoria and Prince Albert bought Balmoral in 1852, he became a favourite of Albert's. And, of course, as the whole world knows, when Prince Albert died in 1861, he became a favourite of hers. John Brown was her personal servant and close friend. Anything else we cannot say for sure but it was an extraordinary relationship between the widowed queen and the hard-drinking, straight-talking Scot. They were the subject of much gossip: she was called Mrs Brown and he was called 'that brute' by her son Edward. Many believed they were secretly married and, supposedly, there is a cache of letters between the two that has been found in Ballater which, if they are ever released, will tell all. But their devotion to each other is well documented. She gave him gifts, including a cottage at Balmoral, and bestowed medals on him. He saved her life at least once and was a constant source of solace and advice. Indeed you could say that he died at the age of fifty-six out of loyalty for, when he was taken ill, some reports say with a cold, others a skin disease that worsened, he refused to take time off. His coffin was taken by train from Windsor to Ballater and then by hearse to Baile-na-Coille, the house the Queen had given him.

In her diary, Queen Victoria only described herself as being 'terribly upset'. But in 2004, a PhD student named

Bendor Grosvenor found a letter from her to a friend, Viscount Cranbrook, in which she tells him about the death. The Queen, who refers to herself in the third person says, 'Perhaps never in history was there so strong and true an attachment, so warm and loving a friendship between the sovereign and servant as existed between her and her dear faithful Brown.' She praised him for his 'strength of character as well as power of frame – the most fearless uprightness, kindness, sense of justice, honesty, independence and unself-ishness combined with a tender, warm heart'. Finally she says, 'The Queen feels that life for the second time is become most trying and sad to bear deprived of all she so needs.' She adds, 'The shock too was so sudden that the Queen is quite stunned.'

After his death, the Queen went into mourning mode as only she could. She commissioned Brown memorabilia, including tie pins and funeral brooches. A life-size statue was erected at Balmoral with an inscription suggested, and probably written, by Tennyson: 'Friend more than Servant, Loyal, Truthful, Brave, Selfless than Duty, even to the Grave'. Apparently she wanted to write his biography but was dissuaded. (Can you imagine?) When she died, eight-een years later, she was buried with, in addition to Albert's dressing gown, a lock of John Brown's hair and his photo in her left hand (artfully disguised by a bunch of flowers so as not to upset the family). She also was wearing his mother's wedding ring.

Queen Victoria was buried in a vast mausoleum at Frogmore in Windsor Great Park. Her statue lies with Albert's, in glori-ous white marble, her skirts flowing, in the centre of royal splendour (though, sadly, also disrepair as the mausoleum hasn't been open to the public, even on the few days a year it used to be, since 2007). You could not find a bigger contrast between that monumental memorial and the weathered gravestone of John Brown in old Craithie kirkyard. It is just down the road from the present kirk (and, conveniently for visitors, the Tourist Information kiosk) that serves the royal family at Balmoral. He lies close to his father.

The golden lettering on the stone is faded but you can just about read that he was a 'beloved friend' of the Queen's. Then she writes, 'That friend on whose fidelity you count, That friend given to you by circumstances over which you have no control, Was God's own gift'. After she died, her son, who became King Edward VII, did his best to erase the memory of 'that brute'. The memorial cairn stone at Balmoral was flattened, his life-sized portrait was sent back to his family, the busts and statues destroyed or moved out of the way. But he couldn't erase the epitaph – or the feeling, as you look at this gravestone, that we don't know the whole story of Mr and Mrs Brown.

## PATRICK DALZEL-JOB

### SOLDIER AND HERO
**1 June 1913–14 October 2003**

*Balmacara New Cemetery, Loch Alsh, Ross-shire IV40*

Name: Bond, James. Height: 183cm, Weight: 76 kilograms; slim build; eyes: blue; hair: black; scar down right cheek and on left shoulder; signs of plastic surgery on back of right hand; all-round athlete; expert pistol shot, boxer, knife-thrower; does not use disguises. Languages: French and German. Smokes heavily (NB: special cigarettes with three gold bands); vices: drink, but not to excess, and women. Not thought to accept bribes.

Ian Fleming, *From Russia With Love*

It is not known if Patrick Dalzel-Job was James Bond but it must be said that the two were never seen in the same room together. Royal Navy Lieutenant Commander Dalzel-Job, who worked for Ian Fleming to go behind enemy lines in the Second World War, could ski backwards, navigate a midget submarine and was a diver and parachutist. He was a crack shot, could blow a safe and survived for a week by himself on an island off Norway, charting German ship movements. Plus, and perhaps this is the clincher, he had a compass concealed in one of his buttons.

Of course, there are a few niggling discrepancies. 'I only ever loved one woman,' noted Dalzel-Job, 'and I'm not a drinking man'. Still, we mustn't let these details get in the way of a good story. It is generally thought that if Dalzel-Job wasn't all of 007 he was at least a 'o' or even the '7'. Another member of Fleming's unit, Peter Jemmett, told a newspaper that colleagues recognised Patrick as the Bond prototype immediately after the first spy novels appeared in the 1950s. 'In contrast to a number of people who have claimed that they were James Bond,' he said, 'Patrick never made any fuss about it'. But nor, it must be said, did he deny it.

He was an only child, whose father was killed on the Somme in 1916. Later, he wrote about when he heard the news:

Mother spoke while continuing to brush her hair and she did not turn round. I was kneeling on the floor on the other side of the bed, playing with some cheap, wheeled toy. It was away from the window and nearly dark there. I looked up and stared for a little while at my mother's back, where the hairbrush moved rhythmically up and down. Then I went on playing on the floor.

This scene feels cinematic, which is a bit of theme with Dalzel-Job. When he was fourteen, his mum took him to Switzerland, where he learned his French, not to mention how to ski. He was fascinated by boats, learning in a flat-bottomed one with a home-made sail, and took a sea navigation course by correspondence. When he and his mother returned to England, they bought a lifeboat and sailed round the Isle of Wight. Their next excitement was to have a sixteen-ton topsail schooner built in Loch Fyne. They set sail for Norway in July 1937. He would spend the next two years learning those waters – and Norwegian. His mother took on a thirteen-year-old girl, Bjorg Bangsund, to help in the kitchen. But when war broke out, he returned to England to enlist.

He was sent to Norway and, in May 1940, when the Germans were driven out of the small Norwegian fishing town of Narvik Dalzel-Job was told to leave the people to their fate. Instead, convinced the Germans would mount a bombing raid, he mobilised a fleet of 200 local fishing boats and organised the rescue of 5,000 people. The next day the Luftwaffe bombed the town, but by then it didn't matter. For his next trick, he had to find a way to escape trial for disobeying a direct order. He hit on the idea of returning to London, accompanied by the mayor of Narvik. 'He got the Norwegian King, who was based in London then, to present him with a medal, so he really couldn't be court-martialed after that,' said his son Ian.

It was after that that he was seconded to work for Fleming behind enemy lines. His first act, after the war, was to return to Norway to look for Bjorg, now aged nineteen. After three weeks, he married her. Obviously this is not the kind of thing that Bond would do, but life doesn't always have to imitate art, surely. I have to say that it felt very dramatic to be looking for his grave. To get there, we drove and drove – in a Honda Prelude, which Bond would not touch, I fear – up past Glasgow, along the snaking shores of Loch Lomond, cutting through the dark majesty of Glencoe, which provided the dramatic setting for the final battle in *Skyfall*. From there we continued up to Fort William, where Dalzel-Job once lived, and on the road to the Isle of Skye.

I had intelligence that he was buried in the village of Plockton, tiny and yet touristy as its location gives it a strange micro-climate in which palm trees thrive. We get to the village, via the sat-nav, on a wiggly little road that would feel dangerous if we weren't looking for Bond. We inspect the graves in the old church. No 007 or even 7. We ask in the trinket shop and then the chip shop. 'He was quite the character,' says the woman dishing up the food. 'I think he's buried in the cemetery out of town.'

So it's back along the wiggly road until it hits the main road, and there is Balmacara Cemetery, with what an estate agent would call stunning views across Loch Alsh to Skye. Everyone knows everyone, even those under the ground, in this part of the world. Some people visiting the cemetery direct us to the south-east corner, greenery all round, flowers in the vase. He shares the grave with his wife, his one love. He is described as 'Knight of St Olav' – very dashing. So I ask the woman I've just met in the cemetery if she thinks he was Bond. 'Only Ian Fleming can tell you that,' she says, smiling. And he isn't talking.

# FLORA MACDONALD

## FOLK HERO
**1722 (date unknown)–4 March 1790**
*Kilmuir Cemetery, near the tip of Trotternish Peninsula,*
*Isle of Skye*

# LEE ALEXANDER MCQUEEN

## FASHION DESIGNER
**17 March 1969–11 February 2010**
*Kilmuir Cemetery, as above*

Flora MacDonald is a heroine of the Highlands, and her name is quite impossible to avoid if you visit the Inner or Outer Hebrides. It was Flora who, as a 24-year-old girl, was convinced that she must aid and abet Bonnie Prince Charlie, the Jacobite Pretender who had fled to South Uist after being defeated at Culloden in 1746. She was an unlikely saviour. Both her fiancé and her foster-father were loyal to the king, but she was told that the escape plan was, indeed, their idea. Thus Flora and the Prince, disguised as Flora's Irish maid, Betty Burke, sailed across the Minch, with a crew of six, evading capture, until landing north of Uig on the Isle of Skye's Trotternish Peninsula. They hid out until he escaped to the island's main town of Portree and, eventually, to France. When they parted, he is said to have given her a locket, saying, 'I hope, madam, that we may meet in St James's yet.' They didn't, of course, but her name, and her bravery, would remain linked forever to his, not least by 'The Skye Boat Song'.

Flora ended up in the Tower for her part in the escapade but lived to tell the tale and return to Skye where she married another MacDonald. She continued to lead the life of an adventuress, heading off to America later for the revolution (on the losing side) before returning, again, to Skye. Myth has it that she was buried in the bed sheet used by Bonnie Prince Charlie (it must have been a trifle frayed) and that her funeral was attended by 3,000 mourners who drank 300 gallons of whiskey. Her epitaph was written by Samuel Johnson, whom she met on his tour of the Highlands: 'Her name will be mentioned in history and if courage and fidelity be virtues, mentioned with honour.'

It's a long drive on a single-track road ('Passing Place' is a sign that you get quite used to on Skye) to Kilmuir Graveyard, eight miles north of Uig and up a hill with jaw-dropping views across the Minch to North Uist and Harris. It is just up the road from the rather humble Museum of Island Life where, as I remember, such items as Flora's egg cup are on view (she really does have something close to cult status here). This is a destination graveyard, visited by tens of thousands over the years. Her original gravestone is now just a lump next to the tall Celtic cross that towers over all, which was put up in 1880 by public subscription.

As we walk up the path to visit Flora and the various other stones here – there is a great one in which the inscription just stops midway, probably because the family ran out of money for the stone-cutter – I see in the new portion of the grave-yard an imposing but graceful slab of slate with the words 'Lee Alexander McQueen' engraved on it. It is so stylish, plus there are the letters CBE after the name, that I just know it has to belong to the fashion designer, the man behind so many brilliant, sexy, wild and exquisite fashion creations, who killed himself, aged only thirty, in London. I walk down to look at the stone, which is rough hewn and somewhat jagged, and on the top of it there is this in white letters: 'Love looks not with the eyes but with the mind.' Below it says 'A beloved son, brother and uncle taken from our lives but never from our hearts.' There are a few (stylish) bouquets, including one with a tartan bow.

I looked up and saw a bus pull into the car park with the words emblazoned on the side: 'WILD AND SEXY'. I must admit that I never thought I'd see a 'wild and sexy' tour at a cemetery. I laughed. I think McQueen would have liked that, though I'm not so sure about Flora. Out of the bus tumbled twenty teenagers and a man in a kilt, who proceeded to trundle by McQueen without a glance and onto Flora, briefly, before heading for the grave of a man who was killed by a boulder that now serves as his gravestone. The man in the kilt tells me that his cemetery tour is 'dead interesting'. I tell you, it's all happening here.

I couldn't quite believe that Alexander McQueen was here. The man who invented the bumster and the skull scarf was, quite literally, cutting edge. He grew up in a council flat in a tower block in Stratford, east London, but, because of his extreme talent for tailoring, ended up rich and famous, the chief designer for Givenchy before he founded his own label. His shows were legendary, involving theatrical and sometimes ghoulish themes. 'God, I've had some freaky shows!' he exclaimed in 2001 after he had a show featuring a naked model in a gas mask inside a glass box filled with moths. But he suffered from depression and died just nine days after his mum. His funeral was in Knightsbridge. But his father came from Skye and this is where his ashes are scattered. And so now, every night, two very brave people, though in completely different ways, not to say ages, Alexander McQueen and Flora MacDonald, get to watch a spectacular sunset together. This may be the most beautiful view of any graveyard in the world.

# DONALD MACMURCHOW

## HIGHWAYMAN AND MURDERER
### Died 1623
*Balnakeil Graveyard, near Durness, Sutherland IV27 4PX*

**B**alnakeil Graveyard is at the end of a road, at the north-westernmost tip of the country, and when you arrive, it feels as if you are teetering on the edge of something quite special. You do not stumble on Balnakeil, you seek it out, and having found it, you don't forget it. It is a destination in itself.

The graveyard is next to a beach, one of those idyllic picture postcard crescents of empty white sands that belong in the tropics but by some twist of fate have ended up in northern Scotland. The views here are of sea, sky, dunes and Cape Wrath. The air is too fresh; the colours are hyper-intense. The imagination runs wild because you feel there is no other choice here.

Balnakeil, or Ba-na-Cille, in Gaelic, means Bay of the Church and there has been a church of one kind or another here since the eighth century. The current one is a dramatic ruined hulk, its roof long gone, its stone walls covered in thick ivy. I walked through what I assumed was the front door and saw, alongside one wall, a strange little stone hut and sarcophagus. This is the grave of Donald MacMurchow, and on the top of the tomb, under his name, are a skull and crossbones and the words 'Momento Mori'. Etched over and below is an epitaph which, hard to read, says this:

DONALD MAKMURCHOU HEIR LYES LO

VAS IL TO HIS FRIEND

VAR TO HIS FO

TRUE TO HIS MASTER IN VIERD AND VOE. DMM 1623

The third line, as usually translated, means 'And worse to his foe', with the last line as 'True to his master in prosperity and woe'. Overhead is a carving with an open hand, a ship, a stag and a fish.

These are the only facts I know. All else is legend. It is said that he was a highwayman, a contract killer and, bizarrely, a church benefactor. I imagine him as a Jack Sparrow-type figure, though that is because of the pirate skull on the tomb, whereas he is actually much more reminiscent of the Headless Horseman in *Sleepy Hollow*, which was another Johnny Depp film, though Christopher Walken was the one on the horse. It is said that Donald MacMurchow killed eighteen people and threw them down the blow-hole of nearby Smoo Cave, now a place for tourists but still monumentally impressive.

It is easy to imagine Donald MacMurchow (head attached) at Balnakiel, sitting astride a tall black horse, which is rearing up, hooves pawing the sky, with a raging sea behind (they do not call it Cape Wrath for nothing). Or, at Smoo Cave, throwing bodies (who? why?) into the salty darkness. This is a tale crying out for a tortured back story of some sort, a broken heart, a crushed childhood, a violent upbringing. But – who knows? – it could be that Donald MacMurchow was just a lazy-bones who did his master's bidding because it was the easiest way out.

If only we knew more! 'Ill to his friend and worse to his foe,' says his epitaph. But he could not, surely, be all evil if he ended up here in a church. The myth is that the church didn't want to bury him on sacred ground, but then money – from him perhaps, or his master – changed hands and a deal was done. Donald McMurchow would be buried 'half in, half out' of the church, a compromise in which he would be given some protection from grave-robbers but would, or so it is said, leave his soul exposed, just in case God happened to be looking down.

*C. S. Rolls, St Cadoc's Church, Llangattock-Vibon-Avel, Monmouthshire*

# WALES

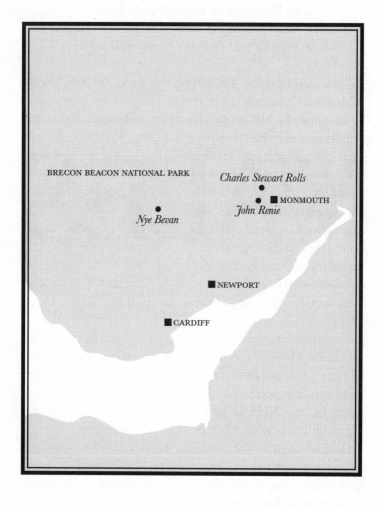

# ANEURIN 'NYE' BEVAN

## POLITICIAN AND FOUNDER OF THE NHS
### 15 November 1897–6 July 1960
*Memorial Stones at Beaufort Road, Tredegar, Blaenau Gwent*
*Ashes scattered near Dyffryn Crawnon valley, Powys*

If you stand on the hill among the giant Aneurin Bevan Memorial Stones, you can choose two very different views. Look down the hill, as he did when addressing thronging constituents over his 31-year period as an MP, and you will see the urban grit and what looks to be the edge of an industrial estate. But look up and you will see hills and sky, which seem bigger than usual. But then, as a politician, Nye Bevan was monumental. He was born in Tredegar, the son of a coal miner who went down the pits himself at age fourteen. Education – and eventually politics – provided his escape. His legendary political career was not without its moments: he was suspended from the party over the Spanish Civil War and from the Commons by the Speaker during a debate on social deprivation. In 1945, he got his chance when he became the youngest member of the post-war Labour Cabinet. He was made Minister for Health, which at the time included housing. Over the next years, he would found the NHS and build some 420,000 homes. He would go on to do many other things but the NHS alone made him a hero – for Labour obviously, but now for all other political parties too.

He died in 1960 and, as in the custom in the Commons, MPs paid tribute to him. 'It seems to me that his death is as if a fire had gone out,' said Labour's Hugh Gaitskell, 'a fire which we sometimes found too hot, by which we were sometimes scorched: a fire which flamed and flickered unpredictably but a fire which warmed and cheered us and stimulated us and a fire which affected the atmosphere of our lives here.'

But it is the words from Conservative Prime Minister Harold Macmillan, who counted the passionate socialist as a friend, which stuck with me. He noted that, when it became known that Bevan had stomach cancer, there had been a huge surge of sympathy for him.

> This feeling was spontaneous and it was shared by men and women of every class and every party, including those whom he had in the past attacked most fiercely. This is perhaps typical of our way of life in this country. Yet it may perhaps be wondered why a man who had been all through his life a somewhat controversial figure should have ended by commanding such general admiration and affection. I think it was perhaps for two reasons. First, he was a genuine man. There was nothing fake or false about him. If he felt a thing deeply, he said so, and in no uncertain terms. If he had some strong opinions, even prejudices, he expressed them strongly but sincerely. Second, he was bonny fighter and a chivalrous one. If he struck blows which sometimes aroused angry reaction, he was always ready to receive blows in return. He sometimes spoke violently; he was never dull. He was sometimes harsh; he was never trite. Finally, he expressed in himself and in his career, in his life, some of the deepest feelings of humble people throughout the land. Unlike many prophets, he was especially honoured in his own country. He was a keen politician but he never played at politics. He was something of a revolutionary. He was always a patriot…

It continues. If you want to be inspired by politics, by what a man as a politician can do, then you could do worse than read Hansard of Thursday 7 July 1960.

It feels as if the world of Westminster was bigger in those days. In death, Bevan returned to Wales forever. He was cremated at Croesyceiliog in Monmouthshire after the simplest of ceremonies, attended by his widow Jennie Lee

MP and about fifteen family mourners. According to *The Times* 'No minister officiated and there were no hymns. After a few minutes of silence part of Beethoven's Sixth Symphony – a favourite of Mr Bevan – was played.' The entrance to the crematorium was lined by hundreds of wreaths, from friends and rivals too. His ashes were scattered above Tredegar near the Duffryn Crawnon valley in the Brecon Beacon National Park. As Michael Foot, his biographer, wrote, 'What he thought about the heart of things must be seen not in what he said and wrote but in his life and death. And it was for sure most fitting that his ashes should be scattered high on the mountain above the Duffryn valley underneath the mountain ash and where the bluebells grew; that was the wild place which, from his youth, he had loved most of all.'

The Duffryn valley is still a wild place and not the easiest to get to by car. We settled for walking along the canal nearby, soaking it all up. Easier to find are the Bevan Memorial Stones, unveiled by Foot in 1972. They are monumental hunks of limestone, the largest one representing Nye himself while the three smaller stones stand for his constituency towns of Ebbw Vale, Tredegar and Rhymney. For walkers this is also the start for the Sirhowy Valley Ridgeway Walk. We visited on a cold spring day, the wind whipping round us, and the whole place felt rather woebegone and forgotten. There is a plaque on the largest stone that says: 'It was here Aneurin Bevan spoke to the people of his constituency and the world', though someone named Chloe has defaced a corner of it with her red graffiti. The spotlights which must have looked up at the stones have been ripped out. There is some desultory rubbish blowing round our feet. On the notice board, there is a fading explanation of who Bevan was. I think it is fair to say that this monument, like parts of the NHS, has seen better days, which is a shame because they do not make them like Nye Bevan any more.

## JOHN RENIE

### HOUSEPAINTER
### 1799 (date unknown)–31 May 1832
*St Mary's Priory Church, Monmouth, Monmouthshire NP25 5HJ*

Just to the side of the pathway that runs in front of St Mary's Priory Church, the calm at the centre of the bustling town of Monmouth, is a large, upright, square stone with a most intriguing 'epitaph' that begs a story…

Once upon a time, in the early nineteenth century, there lived a housepainter here who loved word games.

His name was John Renie and he decided that when he died – and in those days you had to presume that day would come sooner rather than later – he wanted his gravestone to be an acrostic puzzle.

No one really knows where he got the idea but there are plenty of alphabetical acrostics, known as Abecedarius, in the Bible, so perhaps that was his inspiration.

Renie decided to devise a grid, 19 letters across and 15 letters down: right in the middle is the letter 'H', and from that 'H' you can read 'Here Lies John Renie' upwards, downwards, backwards and forwards.

Exactly how many times you can read the epitaph is a matter of dispute but the general consensus is that, if you take in doglegs and zigzags, you can read it 45,760 different ways.

Now I must admit that I have not tested this myself, but as this gravestone was made a Grade II listed monument in 2005, it's not going anywhere and so there is plenty of time to do so.

It is thought that John Renie – who died on 31 May 1832, aged thirty-two – carved the stone himself, or so myth goes; and one theory, by writer and cleric Lionel Fanthorpe, is that the idea was to confuse the Devil in order to ensure his passage to heaven.

Everlasting fame on earth is far easier to judge: certainly John Renie's is, by any standards, a celebrity gravestone.

# CHARLES STEWART ROLLS

## MOTORING AND AVIATION PIONEER
### 27 August 1877–12 July 1910
*St Cadoc's Church, Llangattock-Vibon-Avel,*
*Monmouthshire NP25*

You know his name, or at least his car. This is the man who put the Rolls into Royce. He is buried in the most extraordinarily beautiful place, just over the border into Wales, near Monmouth. This is rolling green countryside, in the foothills of the Black Mountains. Eventually, we find Llangattock-Vibon-Avel but cannot see a steeple. Where, we ask some men at the school, is the church? We find it down a path, past an intriguing old manor house, screened by greenery, and park our car (sadly not a Rolls) amid a flock of sheep. There is birdsong and sheep snuffling, but otherwise, silence. This church is occupied once a month, on the fourth Sunday, for evensong.

Small signs point us towards the Rolls graves, halfway up the slope, away from the church. There are five tombs in all. Charles's is the tallest, a Celtic cross with engravings of a ship and a knight. The first thing you notice is that he died so young, not even thirty-three years old. I sit down here and look out, over the green valley, the white blossom on the tree, the quiet of it all. His grave only identifies him as 'Third Son of 1st Barron Llangattock'. His father, who died after him, is next to him.

Charles Rolls loved speed and danger and motors of all kinds. This is how *The Times* reported his death on 13 July 1910:

> The tragic death of Mr C. S. Rolls yesterday at the
> Bournemouth Aviation Meeting will excite profound sorrow
> and regret not only in this country but wherever men are

interested in the problem of flight. Lord Denham only gave expression to a universal sentiment when in the House of Lords he described Mr Rolls as one of the pluckiest and most skilful of the pioneers of motoring and of the newer and more difficult art of flying through the air. Though prematurely cut off at the early age of 33, he had established for himself a very prominent position not only as a daring and expert motorist and airman, but also as a leading member of a manufacturing firm whose motors embody the highest refinements of technical excellence.

C. S. Rolls could, if he'd chosen, have been a fop or a dandy, a character straight out of *Downton Abbey*. He was born to a life of wealth and privilege but he was obsessed with speed and all things mechanical from a young age. He experimented by concocting various vehicles out of bath chairs and bicycles before turning his attention to steamrollers. 'Never shall I forget my father's face,' he wrote, 'when returning one Sunday morning from church he and the house party with him came upon me driving this ponderous vehicle, black and oily of face but supremely happy.' His nicknames included Dirty Rolls and Petrolls.

The advent of the motor car occurred while he was at Cambridge studying mechanical engineering. He headed straight for France before the Locomotives on Highways Act of 1896 made it legal to use a car on a public road here. Later, he brought back a Peugeot that was the most powerful of its kind at the time. This is his account of his first ride in England:

> As soon as I had started out of Victoria Station, accompanied by a dense mob, I was stopped by a policeman for not waving a red flag. The legal limit of speed in those days was, of course, four miles an hour and two in towns, and each machine

had to be preceded by a man waving a red flag. However, I managed to induce the Chief Constables of Hertfordshire and Cambridgeshire to ask their men to look the other way when I came along and started on this memorable ride. Many and strange were the adventures we had by the way and I and my passengers were utterly exhausted by the time we arrived at Cambridge, having taken 11 hours to do the journey, which works out at an average speed of 4.1 miles an hour.

He pursued his hobby with courage and with the application of an obsessive. 'A man of few words, quiet of manner, and unassuming in disposition, he engaged in undertakings requiring the utmost coolness, self-control and physical endurance,' said his obituary in *The Times*. He entered and won numerous races. For his day job, he sold imported Panhard cars from a showroom in London, as C. S. Rolls. It was during a search for a high-quality alternative that he came upon the name of Henry Royce, a self-taught engineer from Manchester. In 1904, Rolls met Royce at the Midland Hotel in Manchester. Rolls returned to London in a Royce car and soon, with the addition of the all-important hyphen, the Rolls-Royce was born. Rolls was the front man, the seller, the exhibitor. It was at the New York Motor Show in 1906 that he was introduced to the Wright Brothers. Already a keen balloonist, he became besotted with the idea of flying and would say that he preferred being in the air to on the road, as there were no policemen in the sky.

In January 1910, Rolls began to devote all his time to flying. 'On landing we skimmed along the surface rather like a toboggan,' he wrote of his flight in a Wright airplane, 'coming to a standstill a few yards from our starting point. The sensation of flight was novel and delightful and the fact of accomplishing what several eminent scientists have "proved" impossible gave also an added satisfaction.' In June, he purchased a French Wright airplane and, in June, he flew the first double crossing of the Channel. A little more than a month later, he would die at Bournemouth, the first Briton to be killed in an air crash.

Charles Rolls was 6ft 5in. tall and in the centre of Monmouth, not that far from Llangattock-Vibon-Avel, there is a large statue of him, which exudes boyish enthusiasm, for he is holding a model plane. It was paid for by public subscription as a tribute of admiration for his achievements in motoring, ballooning and aviation. It says: 'His death caused world-wide regret and deep national sorrow.' In contrast, Henry Royce would live until he was seventy. He never left the company, working until his death in 1933. He too has a statue but it is outside Rolls-Royce's Derby headquarters, where for years his ashes were kept in an urn.

I went in search of a grave and found a fascinating story of a time gone by, a world without cars, a time when going more than 4mph was intoxicating and when flying was thrilling because you were achieving the impossible. C. S. Rolls's grave may be quiet but his story is full of noise, above all that of engines revving, because that's what he loved.

# AND THE AWARD GOES TO...

*Best Architecture*
1. Julius Beer
2. Sir John Soane
3. William Mackenzie
4. Frederick Leyland
5. Frederick Hitch

*Best View*
1. Flora MacDonald and Alexander McQueen, Isle of Skye
2. The Hancock Family, Eyam, Derbyshire
3. C. S. Rolls, Llangattock-Vibon-Avel
4. Laurie Lee, Slad, Gloucestershire
5. Sir Arthur Conan Doyle, Minstead, New Forest

*Animal Kingdom*
1. Boatswain
2. Copenhagen
3. Athena the Owlet
4. George Wombwell and Frank C. Bostock
5. Charles Cruft

*Heroes and Sheroes*
1. Horatio Nelson
2. Alice Ayres (in Postman's Park)
3. Frederick Hitch
4. Patrick Dalzel-Job
5. Flora MacDonald

*Showmen*
1. Jean François Gravelet or 'Blondin'
2. Joseph Grimaldi
3. Daniel Lambert
4. Marc Bolan
5. André Tchaikowsky

*Inventors*
1. Thomas Crapper
2. George Symons
3. Richard 'Stoney' Smith
4. Frederick York Wolseley
5. Anthony E. Pratt

*Best Epitaphs*
1. Spike Milligan
2. Emeric Pressburger
3. Emily Wilding Davison
4. Ian Fleming
5. Sir Arthur Conan Doyle

*Graves to Eat Your Lunch by*
1. William Blake and John Bunyan
2. Mahomet Weyonomon
3. Postman's Park
4. Willy Lott
5. Thomas Gray

*Sporting Types and Players*
1. Sir Stanley Matthews
2. W. G. Grace
3. Thomas Sayers
4. C. S. Rolls
5. William Mackenzie

*Politicians*
1. Karl Marx
2. Sir Winston Churchill
3. Benjamin Disraeli
4. Nye Bevan
5. Screaming Lord Sutch

*Pioneering Women*
1. Dr James Barry
2. Emmeline Pankhurst
3. Rachel Beer
4. Florence Nightingale
5. Marje Proops

*Graves Touched by Dickens*
1. Pip's Graves
2. Thomas Sayers
3. Jean François Gravelet or 'Blondin'
4. Joseph Grimaldi
5. Thomas Hardy

*Graves of History*
1. The Hancock Family
2. Joanna Vassa
3. William Franklin
4. Mahomet Weyonomon
5. Cross Bones Graveyard

*Regal Touches*
1. King Richard III
2. Thomas Crapper
3. George Wombwell
4. John Brown
5. Daniel Lambert

# ACKNOWLEDGEMENTS

If I could, I would have to list almost everyone I know here, for I have been talking about *Finding the Plot* for years to family, friends, acquaintances and even strangers. When we went to do Emeric Pressburger's grave in deepest Suffolk, we stopped on the way back at a little shop in the village of Debenham. 'What brings you here?' asked the shop owner. 'I'm doing a book on graves you have to visit before you die,' I said. She didn't bat an eye, asked me if I was going to this or that grave before telling me about one in Yorkshire for Donald Duck – not the cartoon but a real person. It is one of the regrets of this book that I haven't included Donald, but the competition was fierce. As I said in the introduction, the first person to suggest this as a book was the former MP (and all round good guy) Tony Wright. I owe a debt to Jeremy Robson, my publisher, who got this idea from the first time I mentioned it, and who has been unfailingly supportive (as well as guiding me to a few of my graves). I also am indebted to everyone who has tramped around cemeteries with me: my mother Beverly Treneman, valiant in sub-zero tempera-tures in wildest East Sussex, and my daughters Gillian Allan and Vanessa Meade, who grew up thinking it not remotely odd to visit graveyards on holiday. My husband, Ian Berkoff, who may not have realised when we got married that he would have to spend his weekends (not to mention holidays) driving to and walking round cemeteries. Others who have contributed graves, essential ideas and encouragement are: Paul Dunn, Jo Balmer, Nancy Treneman, Vicky and Nancy Wilson, Tom Neville, David and Helen Genty, David Robson, Simon Hoggart, Mark King, Torcuil Crichton, Clive and Lynn Rowlands, Camilla Nicholls, Steve and Molly McArthur, Doug and Rose McKenzie. I must also thank *The Times*, both my colleagues and also for its amazing archive. At the Robson Press and Biteback Publishing, I am indebted to James Stephens, Ella Bowman, Sam Carter and Namkwan Cho, who provided essential ideas. Finally, there is John Jensen, illustrator extraordinaire, whose works of art appear through this book and perfectly capture the spirit of this little venture.

# INDEX